GANDHIAN MANAGEMENT

THE PARAGON OF
HIGHER ORDER MANAGEMENT

RAM PRATAP

JAICO PUBLISHING HOUSE

Ahmedabad Bangalore Bhopal Bhubaneswar Chennai
Delhi Hyderabad Kolkata Lucknow Mumbai

Published by Jaico Publishing House
A-2 Jash Chambers, 7-A Sir Phirozshah Mehta Road
Fort, Mumbai - 400 001
jaicopub@jaicobooks.com
www.jaicobooks.com

GANDHIAN MANAGEMENT
ISBN 978-81-7992-959-9

First Jaico Impression: 2009
Seventh Jaico Impression (With New Cover): 2019

In the Memory of
my father Sri S.R. Verma
and
brother Mr. Sri Pratap

✳

ACKNOWLEDGEMENT

It is solely due to the continual persuasion of my wife-Shashi, daughters-Divya and Amrita, and son-Yuvraj, that this manuscript was expeditiously worked upon, and given a final shape for publication.

Over the years, I could not give them their due share in my time, which ethically they should have claimed. I, therefore, express my deep feelings and unfading sense of gratitude to them for giving me moral support in creating this piece of work.

—Ram Pratap

PREFACE

As I perused the voluminous works on Mahatma Gandhi, explored the vast field of his activities, and analysed his life in search for a purpose, I learnt a great deal about him. And as I went in deeper, I got convinced more and more of his eminently high managerial calibre and global management values, which he applied in human resource management and organisational development for constructing a new society of higher order, where ethics and human values find respectable place in interactions and business transactions.

As I continue to elaborate on that in the following chapters, I will gradually drop the word 'Mahatma' pre-fixed reverentially to his surname 'Gandhi'. The only reason being that my intent is to discover in him a facet of managerial feat not yet dealt with by any earlier researcher. This introduction will, I hope, assume great value amongst managers everywhere.

I have sought to throw light on his principles and practices built on his indomitable philosophy of truth, love and non-violence. It is at this juncture that the Gandhian School of Management Thought emerges radically different from any other school of management.

I have quoted, wherever required, views of many thinkers, scholars, managers and humanists-occidental and oriental – from different communities and countries, regions and religions, cultures and customs. Facts and figures have been drawn from major historical events testimonials, meetings, commissions, conferences, UN newsletters, reliable articles, dailies and the books of celebrated authors in global circulation. However, the present analysis represents my own thoughts.

I have, unless unavoidable, refrained from quoting the views of avowed pro-Gandhians in support of his strong points, and also avoided the views of diehard critics obviously to stay out of subjectivity.

I am conscious and aware that even the best analyst or researcher may feel discontented as I do in making presentation on a subject as deep and vast as Gandhi. I may also invite displeasure and incur the dissatisfaction of other scholars on some points of disagreement. If I ever meet or encounter such a predicament, I would not take it by surprise. However, I still hope that readers would find this book novel and interesting, and that the Gandhian School of Management will be accepted exclusively as a new School of Management Thought, worth emulation for making this world a better place, for making corporate management more cognisant of human values and more responsible to social needs.

INTRODUCTION

"Generations to come, it may be, will
scarcely believe that
such a one as this ever in flesh and
blood walked upon this earth"
—Albert Einstein

*

The life of Mahatma Gandhi[1] has always been a classic and exotic subject, of great interest to scholars around the world. They have discussed him in so many ways, in one context or the other, and studied him from so many sources, viz. modern Indian history, British colonial history, his biographies and autobiography, books by renowned authors, journals, and his works (a Government of India publication), articles, special workshops and international or national conferences and symposia. The screening of the feature film *'Gandhi'* directed by Richard Attenborough in the early '80s, and *'The Making of the Mahatma'* by Shyam Benegal in the '90s, brought his life closer to the eyes of the common man. Time and again, Gandhi and his philosophy have been resurveyed, rediscovered and re-institutionalised by the majority of leaders and public figures of most countries across the globe.

Everyone tried and still tries to understand him, and his object-oriented plans and programmes (e.g. newspaper publication in South Africa and India; alignment of Indian diaspora; mill workers issues; conferences and meetings with British emissaries; movements, etc) that he executed at different times through a prismatic vision of one's cultural educational political socio-political, socio-economic, socio-religious and psycho-social backgrounds attached consciously or subconsciously to one's perception. He had been apotheosized as a great spiritual leader – a sage (Mahatma) and ascetic; he had been characterised as a religious and political leader and also an apostle of peace; he had been loved as a surrogate father of the have-nots and underprivileged, and had been acclaimed as the bedrock of India's struggle for freedom. Prof. Gilbert Murray[1], a British classical scholar, extolled him as a 'modern genius of world significance' and that "for every oppressed nationalist in every continent, he became a champion, a matinee idol".

While many historians have accredited him overwhelmingly for India's independence struggle, a few others have criticised and even held him responsible for the partitioning of undivided India, and the mayhem that followed soon after Independence. His followers and admirers include men and women of yesteryears and of present times. They belong to all sections and strata of

---

1. *Mahatma Gandhi - His Life and Ideas'* by C.F. Andrews, p. 191, Reprint 1987, Anmol Publication, New Delhi.

society: middle class, rich, poor, young, old, affluent and deprived, privileged and underprivileged; workers, thinkers, scientists, academicians, administrators, missionaries and politicians.

History has always inscribed their names on its pages and humankind has always bowed before those who abdicated their power and positions, sacrificed comforts, wealth and even their lives for the welfare of society, remedying the cause of hunger, famine, poverty, disease and inequality. Humanity also remembers those who fought incessantly against tyrannies and atrocities. Despite the birth of such great luminaries on this planet, and with millions of their followers and disciples in their time and after, the miseries and woes of the people could not be alleviated, and the conflict of warring nations could not be resolved. This must have impelled Nobel laureate Tagore[2] to express his anguish a decade before the death of Gandhi: "Perhaps he will fail as Buddha[3] failed, as the Christ failed to wean men from their inequities, but he will always be remembered as one who made his life a lesson for all ages to come."

If Mahatma Gandhi's failure on any count is to be gauged against the parameters taken to be the basis of failure in the life of Buddha and Christ, Tagore then does not seem to have meant at all the word 'failure' as used in common parlance, but in an inverted metaphorical sense, it signifies the greatness of these great beings. An appraisal[3] of Tolstoy in the words of Mahatma Gandhi would attest to this very fact: "To say therefore that Tolstoy on his own

2. Rabindra Nath Tagore – a poet and philosopher; he got the Nobel Prize for literature in the year 1913 for his work *'Gitanjali: Song Offering'*.
3. *Young India'*, 20 September, 1928.

admission failed to reach his ideals does not detract a jot from his greatness; it only shows his humility."

Critics who say that Gandhi had failed because he could not avert India's partitioning, and could not prevent communal riots, should recall former UN Secretary General Kofi Annan's bitter disappointment, expressed in the context of the USA-Iraq War of 2003, in a meeting convened at the request of the Arab League and NAM[4]: "All of us must regret that our intense efforts to achieve peaceful solution through this Council did not succeed."

Should that unfortunate cataclysm water down all dedicated efforts that Annan has made for global development and harmony? In spite of this human catas-trophe, the purity of purpose with which the Secretary General has always stood, remains unblemished, and his compassion and increasing concern for global issues are unquestionable. His profound grief for the dead in the UAS-Iraq war and anguish for those living the aftermath, is reflected in his massive efforts in bringing humanitarian aid to the victims and placing responsibility on the UN Security Council for the reconstruction and rehabilitation of post-war Iraq.

It is no revelation that Gautam Buddha, Lord Jesus Christ and Mahatma Gandhi had practised and preached truth, love and non-violence and worked for sustaining human welfare and values, so as to bring harmony, peace and an implicit order in society. They had similar perceptions of the world, and similar prescriptions to eradicate peoples' ills and miseries. But to accomplish their mission, they

---

4. UN News Letters, Vol. 28; 29 March 4 – April, 2003, UN Information Centre, New Delhi.

had chosen different paths, through their unique programmes, methods and means, hoping for a global society – a
world fraternity – to dawn one day upon this Earth.

After all, human life has its own limitations. Any quest,
goal or mission undertaken may remain unfinished,
unattained in one's life span. We work with constraints
and we achieve within limits. There would remain an
epistemological limitation to our understanding of things,
of Nature and of the Universe in an absolute sense as can
be drawn from the Heisenberg's Uncertainty Principle[5] in
quantum mechanics (physics) and Godel's Incompleteness
Theorem[6] in mathematics. Thus, certainty or completeness
in absolute terms in the results of human endeavours has
to be ruled out. 'Limit' is innately associated with man's
reach, still excellence lies in stretching this reach and
narrowing down the gap hereon to absolute perfection.
Hence, there is nothing unusual if the Gandhian model
could cannot resolve all complex human and social
problems in their entirety, but surely, what is unusual, is
that it still holds out a promise for a better world.

Nobel Laureate Physicist Eugene Wigner, while commenting on the Uncertainly Principle of Heisenberg, said that
the hidden variable that does not allow us to reach the
absolute certitude (truth) is the consciousness of a person
(scientist). My own interpretation of the hidden variable
is that it is the ego which cuts into conscience and
interferes with the knowledge and understanding of the

---

5. The principle of uncertainty/indeterminacy, as enunciated by Nobel Laureate
   Werner Heisenberg, mathematical physicist and
   founder of quantum mechanics.
6. Kurt Godel's Incompleteness Theorem: p.250, 'Mathematical Logic'
   by S.C. Kleene, John Wiley & Sons Inc., N.Y.,1967

absolute truth. Truth (reality), non-violence (tolerance) and love (non-prejudice) are organically linked and are the subtle and intrinsic attributes of human conscience, originating in the sub-atomic domain. They play a decisive role in our understanding of 'being', 'seeing' and 'knowing', assuming all other physical conditions, tools and apparatus to be mechanistically perfect. Error means departure from truth, and the scale of departure is the degree of falsity, the severity of which depends on the magnitude of departure that should be observable, measurable and also controllable to a great extent, by a person of higher conscience who may or may not be religious or spiritual.

Gandhi was born in an upper middle class Hindu-Bania (business class) family; Gautam Buddha was a Hindu Kshatriya Prince; Jesus was born of Jewish Mother Mary in impoverished conditions. Each had a different background and different phases of developments, but they all nurtured a common vision. They shared pains, agony, anguish and sorrows with one and all; they were caring, concerning and compassionate having love and sympathy for all; they were kind and considerate, tolerant and forgiving in keeping with the philosophy of non-violence; they were seekers of truth, hence disciplined, determined, and undeterred.

Perhaps to vindicate a universal truth that some core human values and a code of ethical conduct are always essential for our sustainable development and living together, they had come on this earth in different ages, in different societies and in different civilizations, yet they cherished a common goal.

Gautam Buddha and Lord Jesus have been deified and Mahatma Gandhi not yet. Both Buddha and Jesus lived in seclusion, either alone or with their disciples, isolated from common man, but Gandhi lived in the midst of common men. What makes Gandhi essentially different from Buddba and Christ is that: (i) no miraculous incident is attributed to him; (ii) he all alone synthesised truth, love and non-violence into a juggernaut and transformed it into a corporate movement too powerful to be ignored; (iii) Gandhi was determined to empower despondent society and wanted it to be independent, responsive and responsible; and (iv) that he imbibed and upheld reasonable and testable truth ever cherished in Hinduism, Islam and Christianity to enlighten his own conscience, thus creating a separate weltanschauung benevolently interactive with all the communities and people of all kinds.

If Science is nothing but a research for truth, as stated by Nobel laureate C.V. Raman[7], Gandhi is to be regarded as a social scientist, for he never used any ad hoc method in his search for solutions to the problems he encountered in his life. He studied the genesis of problems, the ground realities and legal implications; only then he decided methods and means to attain the goal. Also as a social engineer, he was always reinventing himself and his environment by applying checks and balances to adapt to the changes without changing his rock-solid philosophy. His approach for managing man, machine, materials and methods, were not derived from any legislation, force or fright, but were the distillate of humanitarianism and an

---

7. 'C V. Raman- A Memoir' by A. Jayaraman, p.130, Affiliated East West Publisher Pvt. Ltd. 1989, Madras (now Chennai)

outcome of self-actualisation and introspection sustained by an inner force and inner discipline. He experimented non-invasively on the mind and conscience of the people, ruled and ruling, of two big subcontinents – South Africa (SA) and India, then under the subjugation of the British imperial power.

He wrote in the daily *Harijan*[8]: "Somehow or other the wrong belief has taken possession of us that *ahimsa* (non-violence) is pre-eminently a weapon for individuals and its use should, therefore, be limited to that sphere. In fact this is not the case. *Ahimsa* is definitely an attribute of society. To convince people of this truth is at once my effort and my experiment."

Without any official position and power, he remained an unchallenged and unmatched leader who controlled the psyche of millions of people from all rungs of the society, soliciting their unflinching support for about half a century. After all, plans are not made in a huff and success is not achieved in a jiffy. It takes decades to build a society and centuries to stabilise a nation. Since his struggle was against imperialism and the abuse of imperial power, it was simply impossible for anybody to mark a beginning or perceive an end. Though the field of his operation was complex and vast, he still demonstrated an exceptional managerial prowess and a unique managerial finesse.

His indefatigable work in South Africa which lasted for two decades, sowed the seeds of strong will in the natives and immigrants to unite and work with zest and zeal, and grit and guts for securing their fundamental rights and

---

8. *'Harijan'*, 25 August 1940.

restoring human dignity. Ultimately, the day came and Nelson Mandela took over in 1994 as the first black President of independent South Africa. On being honoured with the Bharat Ratna award in 1990 by the Government of India, Nobel Laureate Mandela said: "The policies of Mahatma Gandhi are much more relevant even today."

After returning from South Africa (SA) in 1914, Gandhi tested his philosophy in his own homeland, India, and used his managerial acumen to lead masses and activate mass movements many a time. The impact of his persona was so deep and irresistible that it changed the mindsets of the people not only of this country, but of the world at large. He showed them a new method of non-violent and non-invasive management, and how to settle differences and grievances through dialogue, persuasion and passive resistance. Oliver Wendell Holmes of the Medical School at Harvard encored: "What another man has taught as a personal discipline, Gandhi has transformed it into a social programme for the redemption of the world."

Curt Coffman, American co-author of the best seller *'First Break all the Rules, What the World's Greatest Managers do Differently'* — said at the Smart Talk (organised by *Hindustan Times* on August 13, 2003 in New Delhi) that great managers are people like Katherine Graham (Chairman, Executive Committee, *Washington Post*), Bill Gates (Chairman, Microsoft) or Mahatma Gandhi. His statement distinctively underlined Mahatma Gandhi as a great manager of very special class.

Dispelling contempt for the past, and dispensing with the arrogance of the present, if we look without prejudice into the gestalts of Gandhian management, the world can still learn a few very important lessons to avoid pitfalls, and avert crisis and catastrophe in the future.

CONTENTS

THE KERNEL OF GANDHIAN
MANAGEMENT

I

"The earth is sustained through Truth."
—Atharva Veda 14-1-1

"The Vedas, I feel convinced, will occupy scholars for centuries to come."
—Prof. Max Mueller

"Let there be no compulsion in the religion, Truth stands out clear from error".
—Koran

"Truth is difficult to listen to, more difficult to speak, and most difficult to practice, though it is simplest, purest, and clearest since it is irreducible, irrevocable and irreversible."
—The Author

*

The bedrock of Gandhian management is the Gandhian philosophy, which is a monolithic structure of truth, love and non-violence. Gandhi applied his philosophy as a litmus test to confirm his principles, and as a fire-test to warrant his practices. It is the integration of this philosophy with his principles and practices that adds a new dimension to the field of management. It defines a new set of management values and hence a new school of management thought.

Most corporates and competing institutions often issue their mission statements in which they declare their philosophy by defining their identity and stating in broad terms their intent or goal, competitive edge or strength, target groups and markets.

IBM aims at supplying intelligent information, hence their innovations give foremost consideration to accuracy, quickness, compactness and security which are crucially important in making decisions in a competitive environment. Microsoft overcomes the barriers of languages by stressing on research and development in many such softwares that are user-friendly and which use symbols and icons to convey similar meanings in different languages. It has, therefore, gained worldwide acceptability and popularity.

Nokia cell phones are 'connecting people', and BPL is 'believing in the best'. Johnson & Johnson promotes its baby products with an accent on body care 'with tender love'. Sony believes in people-oriented policies so that a person hired by an organisation can be accepted as a whole and is not dichotomised in virtuous-self and vicious-self. The Tatas, leader in the Indian automobile sector, combine robustness with sophistication. The Birlas promote their products through cultural and religious activities. Bajaj Auto advertises its products with focus on family happiness and togetherness.

Gandhi, too, carved a philosophy, which he nurtured and upheld throughout his life, only to be known later as Gandhian philosophy. The importance of the human factor in contemporary management can be seen in its finest form in Gandhian management. His humanitarian canvas was so global, and clarion call for natural justice was so intense, that he became an institution by himself much before the world discovered this reality.

The three cardinals of Gandhian philosophy, truth, love and non-violence, are so coherent, cohesive and co-focal, that all together they stand like a solid rock. The absence of even one breaches the wholesomeness of the structure. However, all these elements ought to be understood across a much wider plane and in a much deeper sense beyond the threshold of their common meaning.

Truth is difficult to listen, more difficult to speak, and most difficult to practice, yet it is simplest, purest, and clearest since it is irreducible, irrevocable and irreversible. Knowing 'truth' means knowing the 'reality'. Humans by nature are truth seekers, and they have always been inquisitive, investigative and argumentative to probe more than what they know, to go deeper than what they see in themselves, others and their surroundings, and anything else with which they can interact through physical senses and mental processes. Truth is the aim of a scientist; truth is the goal of judicature; and, for a saint or a prophet, truth is the name of God. But certain parameters, which decide the end results, should also be checked out before arriving at the truth; and they are: credibility of an analyst or experimenter, dependability of an instrument or technique and the reliability of the data from primary or secondary sources. If all these parameters are bias-free and error-free, they add credence to the results that can be accredited as 'true'. However, our access to the 'absolute truth' may still be denied by Nature, for our understanding of 'being', 'seeing' and 'knowing' of the minutest object and event (shorter than a femto-second) – the building block of this universe – has been so far very limited. Such limiting zones are formed in our thought process alone, because the evolution or dissolution of our mental fields effected by internal and external stimuli, defines our analytical power and comprehension up to a certain point of accuracy, beyond which uncertainty becomes larger than the observable object or events of the micro-domain. If we accept it as an inherent limitation imposed by Nature in reaching the ultimate truth, Gandhi must then be regarded as one of the greatest corporate managers and human resource developers of the twentieth century. Or as Nobel Laureate Rabindra Nath Tagore famously said, "He was a living truth at last, and not only quotations from books."

Gandhi knew that common masses cannot manage themselves for perfect non-violence, and elements of imperfection are unavoidable. That is why Professor Gene Sharp[1] of Harvard University argues that according to Gandhi, although imperfection in practicing perfect non-violence is inevitable, one's duty is therefore to strive constantly for the least imperfection.

---

1. '*Non-violence: Moral Principle or Political Technique*' by Gene Sharp, an article from the book '*Mohandas Karamchand Gandhi*', Editor, Verinder Grover, p 60., Deep & Deep Publication, 1998, New Delhi, India.

The second element of the Gandhian philosophy is love, which too has varied meanings and shades in different societies, and for different groups of people. One may instantly relate it to liking, fondness, passion, infatuation, attachment and adoration whereas, in Gandhian context, we must expand its horizon to encompass compassion, empathy, sympathy, kindness, reverence, esteem and devotion. We need to transform our mind-set from passion to compassion, from antipathy to empathy and from individuality to plurality in order to understand the expounded meaning of love.

The third important element of his philosophy is non-violence. Which does not only mean non-killing, non-aggression or non-injury, but also being free from prejudice, jealousy, hatred, animosity, pride and ego, since these elements too implicitly cause some kind of perturbation, a sort of violence towards one's self or others. As a researcher in the fields of science and management, I have always experienced, be it with myself or my peer group, that presence of the above said elements inhibit the recognition of truth in others' work, and create hurdles in searching for the truth within and assessing oneself truthfully. Truth and science, hence scientific management, are closely linked to each other.

Nobel Laureate C.V. Raman[2] meticulously draws a semblance between truth and science: "Science is nothing but a research for truth. Truth not only in the physical world, but in the world of logic, psychology, behaviour and so on. The virtue of a truly scientific frame of mind is the readiness to reject what is false and untrue." We know as

---

2. *'C.V. Raman: A Memoir'* by A. Jayaraman, op. cit.

well from our exercises in the pursuit of science that fear, fright and coercion also strongly interfere in the process of finding truth as they also create perturbation, distort our perception and delude our findings. What one logically deduces is that for scientific management, a manager has to manage the affairs of an organisation without ego, pride, predilection, prejudice, jealousy, hatred, coercion, fear etc., because they all reflect violence in one form or the other.

Hence, the absence of truth and love on any pretext, and/ or the presence of 'violence' in any form would interfere with **SWOT** analysis and **PEST** analysis, and would jeopardise the setting of **SMART** goals, while all these are, in fact, important tools of organisational management. It is ironic that Gandhi has been often misquoted by a few critics as a symbol of 'weakling' and has been mistaken as failed, because they measured his success with a narrow and myopic view arrested within the frame of material gains and gratifications. What they failed to notice is the paradigm shift that Gandhi actuated in human resource management — the very basis of modern corporate management.

At the Millennium World Peace summit held at the UN headquarters, New York, in the last week of August, 2000, about 1,500 religious and spiritual leaders from 75 faiths and 92 countries assembled (as reported by media) and unequivocally affirmed the dire need to establish peace and harmony in the world. They condemned violence and

---

SWOT : Strength, weakness, opportunities and threats

PEST : Political, economic, social and technological environments

SMART: Specific, measurable, achievable and time-bound

issued vigorous statements[3] on the subject 'Towards A World Movement For Non-Violence'. Betty Williams, the Nobel Peace Laureate from Northern Ireland, stressed in her speech that practicing non-violence is not for the faint-hearted, as it requires exemplary courage. Ela Gandhi, granddaughter of Mahatma Gandhi and member of the South African Congress, reiterated: "Non-violence is not a passive concept but an active one-one that demands courage and love, not hatred."

We don't really know how sincerely and seriously the people who participated in this summit have pledged and committed themselves to Gandhian philosophy and to propagating the concept of peaceful co-existence on earth. But we expect that futurity shall respect, more than ever before, the men and women who possess these attributes. Society shall always admire those who can show even moderate sense of respect for truth, love and non-violence.

To corroborate this conjecture, let's recall an incident at the White House at the turn of the century. How narrowly did former President Bill Clinton escape the political disaster during his last tenure! What factors have contributed in bailing him out? His alleged affair with intern, Monica Lewinsky rocked the Presidential Office and the news made headlines in all leading newspapers and magazines. In this sensational case, the issues related to truth, love and non-violence (tolerance) were found surfacing very frequently and were noticed prominently in almost all the meetings and proceedings of Prosecution and Defence.

---

3. *The Times of India*, 31 Aug., 2000.

President Clinton, in a philosophical mien, exclaimed[4] under oath: "It is in the hands of the Congress, and the people of this country, ultimately in the hands of God." Behold, the President did not outright controvert the truth; he did not deny his love; and he did not resort to retaliation or counter allegation (a form of violence) against his adversaries and their accomplices who chose to disrupt his career, disgrace his image and bring discord in his family life. Only simple modesty on the part of Clinton, implying respect for all three cardinals of Gandhian philosophy, swung the public opinion poll as conducted by market research groups, in his favour, exonerating him of his misdemeanour — if it was — and endorsing his continuance in office. Even the later impeachment move against him failed in the U.S. Senate.

It is also worth noticing here how emphatic Henry Hyde, Chairman of the judiciary committee of the US House of Representatives, had been about searching truth alone. He told the House in this context: "We do not make any charges, we simply begin the search for truth." One also sees there an event with a strange coincidence of time and place, when American congress took a historic decision to erect a memorial of Mahatma Gandhi in Washington D.C., and President Clinton accorded his approval on Oct. 28, 1998.

I have purposely brought in here this specific reference to the case of Bill Clinton. Americans have always been interested in the philosophy and methodology of Gandhi as much as Gandhi had faith in their capability to understand and respect human values. He[5] once said; "I am

---

4. *The Times of India*, Dec., 1998.

interested in the United States and in Americans always. There is a special bond of sympathy between us, I believe. The Americans can understand our desire for independence.'

The laws of truth are global; suppression of truth always caused upheavals in public and politics, while just reverence or reconciliation with the truth very often settled down the storm of war and the heat of destruction. Gandhi[6] once said: "Politics bereft of religion is death trap." Religion to him was first humanity and omnipresent God, while God for him was another face of the truth.

---

5. 'Mahatma Gandhi: Letters to Americans', compiled and edited by
Dr E.S. Reddy, Bhartiya Vidya Bhawan, 1998, Mumbai

6. Young India, 3 April 1924.

THE CARILLONS OF
SUPER LEADERSHIP

2

"The whole of Gandhi's life is a fascinating study in the
art of influencing the masses, and by the success he
achieved in this mysterious domain, he must be
accounted as one of the greatest artists in leadership of
all time. He has a genius for acting through symbols
which all can understand."
—Press Attaché of Lord Mountbatten,
last Viceroy of India

"Mahatma Gandhi had immense capacity to go
against odds that made him a great leader"
—Tom Peters

*

1. LEADERSHIP TO SUPER LEADERSHIP – ONE MAN BOUNDARY FORCE

Distinct leadership qualities as seen in different
classes of leadership and pointed out by most
thinkers are – (i) integrity (ii) endurance (iii)
courage (iv) will-power (v) emotional stability (vi) moral

qualities (vii) intellectual capacity (viii) people-friendliness (ix) decisiveness and (x) peer-consultation. Numerous instances in Gandhi's life demonstrate an infallible presence of all these qualities in him. No better example can history cite of a person, other than Gandhi, who had possessed not only all the above said traits of leadership, but also the rare attributes of superleadership.

A leader, according to George R. Terry, should be able to induce masses to follow him or her willingly, while Hodge demands a leader to have the ability to change the attitude and behaviour of others. If both attributes are fused together, it should mean that a leader is capable of infusing people with willingness for change as visualised by him or her, and change is reflected correspondingly in their attitude, behaviour, approach and actions.

Gandhi fit perfectly into the above said format of leadership. When he gave a call, people gathered in multitude; when he walked, millions lined up along his route; when he grieved, millions put their heads down; and when he went on a fast, millions skipped their regular meals. The sacrifices of people who fought against injustice unto their last breath with utmost restraint, and undeterred by suppressive and coercive methods of the ruling government, unquestionably testify their attitudinal transformation brought about by this unsurpassable leader.

"Leadership is influencing people to follow", maintain Harold Koontz and Cyril O'Donnell who wrote 'Essentials of Management'. However, they do not elaborate on how to influence. Should it be done with pomposity, verbosity and falsity, or with veracity and sagacity? Gandhi, with the latter two, and his simplicity, made an everlasting impression on the masses, and with austerity and tenacity fought incessantly against his granitic adversaries. Speaking on 'leadership', international business manage-ment guru Tom Peters[1] recalled Mahatma Gandhi as someone who had immense capacity 'to go against odds', which made him a great leader. Never before or after him could any other leader provide such a single-window super-leadership.

Whether the faith of his millions of followers reposed in him, multiplied his inner force and charged him to a high human potential, or his own copious inner force attracted millions into his aura, is rather difficult to analyse. But he and his followers definitely constructed a feedback loop of will-power where both were reinforcing and energising each other constantly. Lord Mountbatten[2], the last Viceroy of British India, once aptly remarked about his stature and charismatic personality as 'one-man boundary force' — a rare tribute bestowed upon any world-class leader.

2. THE REVOLUTION MAKER

To guard against abuse of power and authority by a person, group, organisation or government, the common man has always appealed, through ages, in despair or hope, to the justice-dispensing authorities. Nearly all revolutions, political upheavals and constitutional settlements that history has chronologically recorded around the world in the last millennium, took place against this abuse, which perpetrates human indignity and human rights violations.

1. India Times Strategy Summit, 29. October 2002, Hyatt Regency, New Delhi

2. *'Gandhi: A Life'* by Krishna Kriplani p.179, National Book Trust, 1985, New Delhi.

Magna Carta (1214) – the English political charter-pruned the authority of royal power; the American War of Independence led to the Declaration of Independence (1776); the French Revolution (1789-1799) overthrew the feudal structure of the French society; the Russian Revolution (1917) fractured the tsarist regime and transferred power into the hands of the Bolsheviks; and India's struggle for Independence (1947) from the shackles of the British Empire made global impact. All these are testimonies to the victory of the common masses and mass movements. Leaders of these mass movements changed the course of history, becoming idolised as the revolution-makers of their times. Gandhi, too, led many mass movements successfully, and proved to the world that there is a powerful weapon of truth, which, if used non-violently, can fight out the misrule and wipe out an unworthy government.

The United Nations has been pleading for long with all nations to take necessary measures for the protection of human rights and propagation of human values. Human rights awareness is surely most important for all societies, but people also need to bear in mind that the epithet 'protection of human rights', is neither used as a deceptive hoax for obstructing and dampening of the judiciary process in the trials of heinous criminals or terrorists, nor is it used for cushioning a verdict of the Court of Law.

3. MASS MOBILISATION

World history would miss a great deal both in essence and in the spirit of mass movements, if it misses to mention Gandhi and his unique philosophy and methodology of mass mobilisation. During his public life spanning over twenty years in South Africa (SA) and over thirty years in British ruled India, most of the issues that he addressed were related to humanity and humankind. Gandhi led many mass movements, but only when convinced of the purity of purpose and parity of thoughts and action of the people involved.

The quality of superleadership in the leaders of mass movements has to be assessed not only by the magnitude and intensity of mass mobilisation, but also by the propriety of means and methods used in mass movements. All mass movements effectuated by Gandhi made a lasting impact worldwide and had an exceedingly large number of followers from all society stratas. The Press Attaché[3] of Lord Mountbatten, while wrapping up the history of British Colonial rule in India, wrote in 1947 a classic note in his diary: "The whole of Gandhi's life is a fascinating study in the art of influencing the masses, and by judging the success he achieved in this mysterious domain, he must be accounted as one of the greatest artists in leadership of all time. He has a genius for acting through symbols which all can understand."

Two events cited below should confirm that true leaders can draw an unconditional support of the masses and can rock even a big empire if they take up the responsibility and commit themselves to serve humanity.

(A)   The Cape Union Supreme Court[4] ruled on March

---

3. Ibid. *'Gandhi - A Life'* p.188.
4. *'Mahatma Gandhi - A Chronology'* Compiled by K.P. Goswami., Publication Division, Ministry of In formation and Broadcasting, 1971, New Delhi.

13, 1913, that only Christian marriages were to be considered legally valid. Non-Christian and non-registered marriages stood virtually nullified. Since registration of marriages in Hindu and Muslim communities was not a common practice then in India, the decision of the Court denigrated many wives and children as illegitimate. This was a political move to prohibit Indians from bringing in their families and settling, but it was also grossly humiliating, with increased vulnerability of ripping the social and economic fabric of Indian diasporas. It was easy to switch on spark, but most difficult to bring its fire under control.

Gandhi's capability to channelise people's anger through mass movements and protests with minimum collateral damage, arouses as much inquisitiveness as his capability to mobilise masses. The purpose of civil disobedience as Gandhi perceived it is not to destroy a person, but to abolish an institution or system that works against human values and humans. To convey this perception by the meaning of the term apparently borrowed from the essays of Count Leo Tolstoy, he even preferred to use the phrase, 'civil resistance' instead. He thus analysed the purpose of civil disobedience[5]: "There is a danger in civil disobedience only because it is still only a partially tried remedy and has always to be tried in an atmosphere surcharged with violence. For when tyranny is rampant, much rage is generated among the victims. It remains latent because of their weakness and bursts in all its fury on the slightest pretext. Civil disobedience is a sovereign method of transmitting this undisciplined, life-destroying latent

---

5. *Young India*, 27 March 1930.

energy into disciplined life-saving energy whose use ensures absolute success." Deeply aggrieved over the order passed by the Cape Union Supreme Court undermining the sanctity of Indian custom-based marriages, Gandhi organised in protest a large-scale civil disobedience (satyagrah) across the provinces of Transvaal and Natal. Coalmine workers of Newcastle also joined the strike, and women workers, hitherto inactive, participated vigorously in the movement. Mass mobilisation was witnessed on an unprecedented scale. About 50 thousand indentured labourers refrained from work and supported the satyagrah. The police failed to anticipate the extent of furor and commotion, which the participation of women and the arrest of Gandhi would add to the movement. On November 6, 1913 Gandhi[6] was the first to be arrested there. In early 1914, negotiation between General Smuts and Gandhi started and an agreement was soon reached. Under the Indian Relief Bill[7], later to become law, marriages of Hindus, Muslims and Parsees were pronounced legal.

(B) The British Administration in India monopolised making and selling of salt under the Salt Law, prohibited all others from doing so and made buying from the Government compulsory. To maintain fixed prices for a stipulated profit margin, the Government often destroyed the surplus salt that could not be sold profitably.

---

6. 'Mahatma Gandhi - A Great Life in Brief' by Vincent Sheean, p.70, Third Print, 1982, Publication Division, Ministry of Information and Broadcasting, Government of India, New Delhi.

7. Ibid, p.72.

While salt is a basic ingredient for food, it is sometimes even a substitute for vegetables and pulses, especially for workers and peasantry. The restriction imposed on free selling, making or buying of salt was a condemnable act by the Government. The human indignation perpetrated through a grain of salt, jolted the very soul of every Indian and drew attention of human rights activists from all over the world. Gandhi tried all means and methods to persuade the Government to review this law, to no avail. He was left with no other choice but defy the Government openly by embarking upon civil disobedience to register his protest and solicit the co-operation of millions of people across the world. In modern Indian history, this famous event is recorded as the Dandi March that he undertook from Sabarmati Ashram to the Dandi sea cost. Upon reaching there on April 5, 1930, he picked up a handful of salt from the seashore, thus breaking the law. Let's attribute to this simple action Neil Armstrong's words, spoken during his moonwalk in 1967: "It was small step for a man, but a giant leap for mankind". This was the beginning of the countdown in the meltdown of the British colonial rule in India.

4. PRIMUS INTER PARES

The man who treated all men as equal, had no equals to match his qualities of leadership. He showed that the enduring leader is one who is not a superior person, but only first among equals: first to abide by the moral code of conduct; first to bear the brunt of change; first to surrender privileges, and first to sacrifice one's life. A leader is elected and chosen to serve, and not installed to rule. For him/her, an organisation is like a marigold, of which every petal is a complete flower in the functional sense, and still a part of the full composite flower. "The movement is based on the faith that when a whole nation is roused and on the march, no leader is necessary", said Gandhi[8].

5. SAVOIR FAIRE

Gandhi's ability to deal with a wide range of societal and political issues, and his capability to offer a viable solution was amazing; his patience was unfathomable and tolerance impregnable. His interaction with people at all levels and in all sections of society was so close and regular, that he developed a deep understanding of different stimulus-response (S-R bonding) patterns of various groups in society, and his through and through involvement from the concept to launch phase of mass movements, made him a master of group dynamics. He knew that disparity due to differences in wealth and wisdom would continue, but he was well convinced that by one's sacrifice and dedication, it would not be difficult to form a cohesive group of people ready to come forward and work for the protection of human rights and dignity.

Great leaders are not necessarily good managers, and great managers are not necessarily good leaders, but here was this great being that was a synthesis of both. There was in him a confluence of many attributes such as moral, ethic, truth, love, non-violence on the one hand and courage, action, determination, transparency and sacrifice on the other.

---

8. *Young India*, 3 April 1930.

In a letter dated January 11, 1928 from Allahabad, Pt. J .L. Nehru – who later took over as the first Prime Minister of independent India – wrote[9] to Gandhi: "I felt and feel that you are infinitely greater than your books. Above everything I admire action and daring and courage, and I found them all in superlative degree in you. And I felt instinctively that, however much I may disagree with you, your great personality and your possession of these qualities would carry us to our goal".

When Gandhi quoted from the Gita, the Koran or the Bible, he was a missionary. When he initiated compromise between the two opponents, he was a mediator. When he applied his trident of truth, love and non-violence, he was an uncompromising autocrat. When he gave procedural details to accomplish a goal, he was a bureaucrat. And when he delegated power to his colleagues or juniors, he was a trainer and developer.

6. CONQUERING FEAR AND HATRED

Reminisces Prof. Chandrasekhar Rao[10], former Director, Commonwealth of Learning (COL),Vancouver, Canada: "As the President of Indian Society of the London School of Economics, during my own Ph.D Programme in the late 50s, I had thought of extending an invitation to Sir Winston Churchill to grace the Society's function as chief guest on Indian Republic Day, for which I sought a meeting with the former by an appointment at the

---

9. 'The Collected Works of Mahatma Gandhi', p. 543 Vol. XXXV, Publication Division, Ministry of Information and Broadcasting, Government of India, New Delhi.

10. Private Communication, March 1999.

Atheneum Club." Churchill, however, regretted his
inability to come to the function and remarked impishly,
"Indians wouldn't mind missing me on this day". Well-
known in his friends' circle for his witty and extempore
comments, Prof. Rao spoke to Churchill: "Sir, it is a fact
that there has been a wide divergence in your
understanding of India and our own perception. More than
this, a certain sense of harshness characterised our mental
perceptions. But then that happens in every country in the
context of national struggle. After the struggle ends,
perceptions begin to change. You, yourself, had said in
1949 – when Pt. Jawaharlal Nehru persuaded India to stay
in the British Commonwealth – that you had heard of
persons conquering fear and hatred but not experiencing
them, and that Nehru's action was a vindication of that
saying. But, Sir, Nehru here too was a follower of
Gandhi*ji*." In fact Pt. Nehru at this juncture upheld only
Gandhi's views and reflected them in his foreign policy.

Nehru, who transferred his political dependence largely
onto Gandhi and has been described as his protégé, was at
times also critical of him, but still subdued to his
Gandhi's persona. In a letter[11] dated January 11, 1928 and
sent from Allahabad, Nehru wrote to Gandhi: "I have
asked you many times what you expected to do in the
future and your answers were far from satisfying [...]
faith in your amazing capacity to bring off the improbable
kept us in a expectant mood [...] You misjudge greatly, I
think, the civilisation of the West and attach too great an
importance to its failings [...] You have criticised strongly
the many obvious defects of industrialism and hardly paid
any attention to its merits."

---

11. op. Cit. *The Collected Works of Mahatma Gandhi'*.

In his response through a letter[12] dated January 18, 1928 from Sabarmati Ashram, Gandhi's reaction was nonchalant but challenging without any trace of disdain and fear of losing a great admirer in this rising leader of India:

"I see quite clearly that you must carry on open warfare against me and my views. For, if I am wrong, I am evidently doing irreparable harm to the country and it is your duty after having known it to rise in revolt against me. Or, if you have any doubt as to the correctness of your conclusion, I shall gladly discuss them with you personally. Write me a letter for publication showing your differences. I will print it in *Young India* and write a brief reply."

7. GLASNOST

"What I practice is what I preach (WIPIWIP)" has to be the motto of a leader or head of an organisation, group or a country; only then the people can repose faith in him. Contrary to the prevalent myth that strategy cannot be made transparent, and transparency cannot hold strategy, Gandhi always adopted transparent strategies. Look at his methodology while dealing even with his adversaries: he would speak truth forthright, execute his plans openly, and would leave it to the opponents to take any course of action which the latter deemed fit to thwart his plans.

8. ESPRIT de CORPS

Team spirit has to be promoted so that the efforts of all members of a team converge synergistically to produce desired results. Each member of the team has to pay due

---

12. op. Cit. *The Collected Works of Mahatma Gandhi*.

respect to leadership and has to acknowledge the supremacy of the organisational goal, otherwise no democratic
set up or parliament of any government can function even
for a day. In realising the object of an organisation or
team, members may also have to sacrifice a part of their
personal freedom, privileges and accolades.

In the initial phase of his public life in South Africa,
Gandhi was often hamstrung in organising mass
movements owing to lack of esprit de corps among the
people. The obvious reason was that the majority of Indian
diasporas in South Africa comprised heterogeneous groups
of Hindus, Muslims and Parsees working in different
occupations (traders, businessmen, workers or labourers),
and originating from various parts of India. However,
Gandhi discovered a common thread: all immigrants were
subjected to perpetual subjuga-tion and humiliation by the
local British authorities, and were abhorrently denied
equity and equality. He struck their conscience by asking
them to rise above petty differences, interests and
maligned squabbles, and not to confound their goal-fight
against unjust and inhuman treatment.

At this juncture, a laudable comment of Imran Khan — a
legendary Pakistani cricketer of yester-years on team spirit
and leadership irresistibly flashes in my mind. Ten Sport
channel, on 30 March 2004, was airing the India-Pakistan
third day test match on Multan ground. When I switched
on the TV, I found the live telecast interposed with a
group discussion among great cricketers of their times —
Manjareker and Siddhu from India, and Khan from
Pakistan. Incidentally, Manjareker touched a sensitive point
as to why the Indian captain brought the first innings to
an abrupt close, when a stupendous score of 675 for 5 was

already reached and well-known ace batsman Tendulkar was stranded at 194, just 6 runs short of double century, even though there were about 16 overs to go. Imran Khan gave a candid remark instantly: that it is fatal thinking to focus on an individual's milestone, when the aim of the team is to win, and the captain is to decide a strategy. At the close of the match on day 5, when India won the test match, Imran Khan's thoughtful words were proven to be true in this event watched by millions of viewers around the world.

9. UNIVERSAL VALUE SYSTEM

The intersection of value sets of all those great legendary figures who came to this planet in different times and opposed the demonic and destructive forces in societies and thus literally saved humanity from coming be extinct, is not a null set. The intersection contains such elements as truth, love, tolerance, non-violence, equity, equality, compassion and concern for others. These are thus to be seen as timeless and borderless values, hence universal. They bind people of all castes, creeds, religions and nationalities. Gandhi re-established them in the modern time and practiced them to resist the wrong.

10. VERACITY AND SAGACITY

Sagacity loses luster if it is not consistent with veracity; a good judgment has to be embedded in truth. A true leader, therefore, takes a decision neither to seek gratification or applause, nor to appease somebody, but to uphold the truth. It is well taken that the judiciary would not ignore facts, statutes, acts, laws, evidences, witnesses and precedents, yet passing of a judgment has to take cognizance of circumstances, motives, means, methods and worth of a person. Gandhi's approach in dealing with any issue on any occasion is seen to combine both the principles of legality and natural justice.

11. GRASSROOTS LEVEL CONTACTS (GLC)

The success of mass movements led by Gandhi shows again the importance and power of GLC to sustain leadership. His constant and empathetic interaction at the grassroots level got him accepted by the people virtually as a member of their families. By distancing himself from the love for comforts of life, he not only identified himself with the conditions of a common man, but also made himself a sensitive receptor of their agonies and distress. For long lasting leadership, it is also necessary that barriers to communication between a leader and common men are broken. A leader has, therefore, to see that not many layers of hierarchy are created between him or her and the people at the lowest rung; and that the people's voice does not go unheard and doesn't get distorted to the extent of even belying the core truth. The political history of the world is replete with cases of leaders overthrown soon after they lost contact with the grassroots level.

Gandhi did not sit in an ivory dome with his coterie around. He was, most of the time, travelling all over the country, even in far flung areas, inhospitable and hostile zones, propagating his message and taking instant feedback from all, including the bottom line. Where he could not reach personally, he still established contact by sending out his notes and writings on issues of local, regional and national importance. For multilingual newspapers, both in South Africa (SA) and India, he wrote editorials on simple to complex issues and clarified his standpoint. He often invited readers' views, and even entertained verbal comments of neo-literates and illiterates.

12. PARTICIPATION

Human resource managers of many companies confirm that employees are much less bothered of their participation in management if the issues in question have no direct impact on their lifestyle and working conditions. But they are hurt deeply and react sharply against those decisions, the fallout of which adversely affect them in terms of their position, promotion, work, working conditions, perks, purse and group interest, if any. It is, therefore, now well accepted that employees' participation in the decision-making process of an organisation is crucially important for its smooth functioning. To institutionalise this concept, many corporates have, therefore, adopted the so called Japanese 'ringi' approach, by which management's views on certain issues are circulated among all those groups which are going to be affected by certain decisions. Comments of the people likely to be affected are solicited to make necessary amend-ments, if required, before the decision is transformed into an effective formal 'office order'. However, the participa-tory 'ringi' approach is often criticised for its slowness. The Gandhian approach tries to provide its remedy. For smooth functioning of an organisation which respects employees' participation, Gandhi advised workers to reciprocate by abdicating part of their freedom and privileges, reposing confidence in the management and authorising them to take final decisions on important and urgent matters. Otherwise, the participatory process might end up in inconclusive discussions and unconscionable delays, where democracy may turn into mobocracy with its serious and untoward consequences.

13. DEVELOPMENT

The good of an individual is contained in the good of all, while the good of all is contained in the good of individuals. 'We are developing', 'we are progressing' and 'we are shining' are often used synonymously, without any regard to the queries 'Who is developing?', 'What is developing?', 'How are we developing?', 'How much have we moved towards our destination?' and 'What means are we using for development?'.

Development is not a one-dimensional process. It is a multidimensional and multilayered growth and progress which has to be sustainable. Progress should take a balanced and holistic view of life and living, while development should facilitate an integrated growth of all individuals and the society. This underscores the need for progress and development in crucial areas like education, health, social security etc. in a compatible and unified framework of needs, opportunities, equity and ethicality.

Gandhi's public life extending over five decades is filled with numerous occasions and umpteen writings, where he laid emphasis on self-discipline, health, education, dignity of labour and service to community – especially the disadvantaged groups, women and children. At many gatherings, he had been emphatic on gender equality, equity and justice. The Phoenix Settlement and Tolstoy Farm in South Africa, and Sabarmati Ashram in India set up by him, are important examples of his major initiatives and concerns for integrated development of both men and women. Market-driven view that industrialisation alone can spurt economic growth and development, is not wholly supported by the Gandhian view of development that focuses first on social reforms, the implementation of which does not require huge investments but only concern, commitments and convictions on the part of the decision makers, managers and also the people.

Millions of men, women and children across the world are often victims of famine, drought, drinkable water shortage, and growing pollution in the local environment. Millions of children are experiencing malnutrition and child abuse, while the elderly are suffering from psychosomatic diseases and have been victims of family neglect, harassment and medical insecurity. A society is obviously in the grip of stark poverty when its people are forced to live below subsistence level as they are denied the right to primary health care, education, adequate housing, and even the right to two square meals and drinking water. If we are developing, why are we seeing such shortages all around? And if we are progressing, why are we seeing exploitation in all sectors, what destinations are we then heading to? Questions remain unanswered even today, when the world has taken leaps in medical sciences, space technology, IT and nuclear armaments. Is that enough?

The UN Commission on Human Rights reaffirmed in the year 2000 that the 'right to development' is an integral part of human rights, In a resolution adopted by consensus, the Commission urged[13] all UN member States "to eliminate all obstacles to development at all levels, by pursuing the promotion and protection of economic, social, cultural, civil and political rights."

---

13. UN News Letter, New Delhi, 15 April 2000.

COMPARE AND CONTRAST WITH
OTHER MANAGEMENT THOUGHTS

"I never think of what I have said before. My aim is not to be consistent with my previous statement on a given question, but to be consistent with the truth As it may present itself to me at a given moment"
—Mahatma Gandhi

"Great managers are people like Katherine Graham (Chairman, Executive Committee, Washington Post) Bill Gates or Mahatma Gandhi."
—Curt Coffman

*

It is not good enough to apply only one model of management to all systems, tasks, situations and environments. While organisations tend to follow different schools of management thought, or their own mix in designing and implementing organisational strategies, the Gandhian management thought stands out distinctly among all.

It is true that Gandhi never owned an enterprise, never held any managerial position and never took formal lessons in management or taught it in any academia. But these are no valid reasons to negate his stature as one of the greatest doyens of management. After all, Thomas Watson (Sr.) of IBM, R.W. Johnson of Johnson & Johnson, Akio Morita of Sony, Henry Ford of Ford Motors, J.R.D. Tata of Tata Group of Industries and Bill Gates of Microsoft had no formal training in management, yet they made a mark in the corporate world and earned recognition worldwide.

Gandhi too contemplated, crystallised and theorised his principles, thereafter drawing up his plans and prog-rammes, which he first experimented upon successfully with small groups, only to finally execute them on a colossal scale. Intriguingly enough, he was mainly comfortable with the most complex branch of management – managing people. About the complexity of human behaviour, Prof. Tom Lambert (1) points out: "People do different things for the same reason, while they are doing the same thing for different reasons." It is really very hard to predict how people would react to different situations and how human behaviour unfolds itself in different circumstances. Gandhi's success in dealing with diverse groups of people, culturally different societies and a wide range of their problems for over five decades, is by any yardstick a vying and unbeaten benchmark for world-class managers.

Gandhian management differs from others in its being, modus operandi, and its social welfare philosophy, where concern for social reforms takes precedence over economic reforms, and where human values remain at the centre stage. In close agreement with Gandhian views, Nobel

Laureate Amartya Sen (2) opined: "Social reforms are not the consequences of economic reforms but economic reforms are the consequences of social reforms." Right to freedom of speech and right to development and equal opportunity for which Gandhi fought throughout his life, form the bases of social reforms and community development.

Commenting on the characteristics of Asian managers, Prof. Gabino A. Mendoza (3) identifies one most important quality of a manager: "He dedicates himself to making continuous enhancement of quality of human life in the society in which he lives [...] No longer does he live only for himself [...] He is a man for others. In short, he is a professional." The life of Mahatma Gandhi is a saga of human endeavours that shaped momentous events and mighty movements, which testify that he was beyond doubt a man for others. He lived his life not in isolation, but in the midst of the masses and for the masses only, uplifting the underprivileged, marginalised and disadvantaged. Virtue lies in sacrifice and greatness in giving. With qualities of virtuous leadership and thoughts of benign sacrifice, Gandhi configured a management construct of higher order that calls attention to searching for truth, invigorating the inner self and listening to the voice of conscience. And this whole exercise can be started off conveniently with a simpler version, by requiring to practise human values in our day to day activities. This makes, in essence, his policies, plans, programmes and practices characteristically of higher order, yet adoptable.

All organisations have their own organisational ethos. The theories of Japanese management give emphasis on staff skill, shared responsibility, super-ordinate goal and 'ringi' approach. The American corporate management lays emphasis on the individual, structure, strategy and system. While the British corporate world (now slowly changing) often focuses on centralised authority, close supervision, rank and file. Gandhi stressed the need for holistic and integrated development of every individual, then the development of community and the development of a welfare state for which he held everyone responsible and accountable. He considered no work as infra-dig and believed that working with dignity should be the only way to make one's work and life dignified, though it is necessary that the allotment of work be done according to the capacity and capability of an individual. He realised that human resources are the fountainhead of all activities, and therefore management must frame people-centric policies, and the State must promote programmes that support the enhancement of human life. His core thesis on issues related to industrial and technological problems always set community development and people's welfare as a high priority item on his agenda.

While Gandhi was working hard to establish order and harmony in the amorphous social matrix of the South African States afflicted deeply with problems of ethnicity, contemporary behaviourists and social scientists like Emerson, Gilbreths, Follet, Barnard, and McGregor, were pleading humanistic approach in the context of organisational administration. Gandhi's approach to correct a delinquent or a criminal is parallel to Douglas McGregor's Human Motivation Theory Y, mainly in the sense that people are basically good, responsible and not averse to work. Therefore, any deviation in normal, good behaviour of a person (if he is not a brute, psychic or a hardened criminal) is the consequence of his ignorance or the circumstantial compulsions to which he succumbs and takes himself to committing offence, blunders and crimes. Rather than, therefore, hating a delinquent or a criminal, it is desirable to effectuate an attitudinal change in the person to abjure crimes.

Gandhi hated sins, not sinners, and despised crimes, not criminals. Some earlier thinkers relied on experience, he relied on truth at the instant. While others resorted to mathematical modelling, he resorted to experimentation. When some viewed management as an analysis, he viewed it as a synthesis. While a few focussed on system approach, he focussed on a holistic approach.

The last quarter of the 20th century took note of the work of few other management wizards – Peter F. Drucker, Edwards Deming, H. Mintzbergs to name a few. The corporate world has come to recognise the role of organisational behaviour and quality management as crucial to the success of an enterprise or an organisation. But it was Gandhi who relied wholly on the intrinsic worth of human capital, and acknowledged this as key factor in all ventures. The lessons of George Elton Mayo – well known for his Hawthrone Experiments (Hawthrone and Western Electric company, Chicago) on productivity and work conditions, and also the philosophy of Mary Parker Follet – a visionary in the field of human relations and democratic organisation can be clearly read in Gandhi's management when he organised groups, held meetings and led movements.

Gandhi also knew that group behaviour and mob reaction do not match with the response and behaviour of an individual. When he could not ensure people's disciplined conduct and attitude to peacefully participate in his movements, without resorting to violence and vengeance, he either called off or procrastinated many nationwide strikes (*hartals*) and events on the eve of the slated day, which he himself had fixed. "We must not think of starting mass civil disobedience unless we are sure of peace being retained...", was his firm reply (4) to the media and other activists who agitated upon him calling off the Bardoli civil disobedience movement (5) in the wake of the clashes between public and police at Chauri-Chaura (U.P., India).

Gandhi preferred granting need-based functional autonomy to an individual, a group or an organization. But at times, he also endorsed some specific decisions taken by the leadership alone, for he knew that group decision may not be fully guarded against arbitrariness, since personal opinion of an influential individual in a group can also, for various reasons, be projected by collusion of some other members as a consensus of the group. Gandhi, therefore, reckoned functional transparency as the primary require-ment in participative and committee management. He was transparent even to his critics and adversaries. His openness to criticism and his constant efforts to reinvent himself, restructure his thoughts and reengineer his plans should be taken as a noteworthy contribution in the evolution of healthy organisational leadership.

Mikhail Gorbachev, former President of the erstwhile USSR, revived this very concept in his policy of Glasnost (transparency and wider dissemination of information) and Perestroika (restructuring of economic and political system). For a commoner in the former Soviet Union, it worked as a great morale booster and in the polity of nations, it created new equations, perhaps because it was a complete reversal of the closed-door political system then prevailing in that country. It may, however, be worthwhile to recall that in contrast to the closed system, Chester Barnard, who gave significant contributions to the theory of organisational structure, fostered, in 1930, an idea of open system theory (6) – a notion that advocates the necessity of dynamic interaction of a system with its environment – which got recognition about a quarter of a century later.

Gandhi was a fervent thinker, a prolific writer, an eloquent speaker, and an excellent communicator. Over and above, he was adept at mass communication and apt at taking feedback. And communication has its unique place in the practice of good management. Chester Barnard had exclusively highlighted the importance of this component. It would be difficult to find in the annals of management history any other case better than that of Gandhi where a man has so exhaustively and meticulously used all means and modes, channels and chains of communication available, in order to reach out to the masses intensively and extensively.

Editing simultaneously many newspapers in different languages and in a hostile regime, must have been an onerous and arduous task. But Gandhi undertook it in all earnestness and carried it on dauntlessly, with full dedication. This testifies that he was convinced of the importance of media and mass communication, and multi-rayed information dissemination. However, he also knew that majority of the populace then in India and Indian diasporas in South Africa were illiterate, hence print media might not be so effective in raising their awareness and responsiveness as to reach the level he wanted it to be. He, therefore, went on touring, meeting people and talking face to face with as many as possible, up to the lowest rung, undertaking journeys by road, train and walking miles after miles.

Gandhi was seriously concerned with the problems of workers and the working class, not because he was against industrialists and industrialization, but because he was against the mechanistic approach of treating humans as spare parts of a machine. With the advent of new technology, new machineries and hence new scientific methods, he held that workers need to be trained and retrained to improve their efficiency and hence productivity on the job; they should not be retrenched or replaced overnight as if they were removable spare parts, and should not be thrown out of the systems like disposable waste. He argued that retrenchment and lay-offs without sufficient and cogent reasons, such as dereliction of duty, would rather aggravate problems.

One should not forget that scientific management pioneer F.W. Taylor (1900) was confronted with irate workers not owing to his scientific manufacturing methods, industrial processes and workers' performance evaluation, but owing to his policy of retrenchment and lay-offs without making provisions for adequate orientation and opportunity for employees for learning, training and retraining. In developing and under-developed countries where copious labour force has always been cheaply available, use of a large chunk of employees' dividends for large scale automation of equipment and machinery to increase production, leaving few on the job and many without it, is not only a rash and irrational decision, but also a social menace – he believed. It was also a need of the time to engage as many workers as possible in the production and manufacturing units. And for supplementing the meager earnings of the workers on agricultural land, he thought it essential to provide them an auxiliary source of earning during idle months of a year. He advised them to make use of an indigenous piece of equipment – the spinning wheel (*charkha*) for weaving yarn and making cloth.

In the matter of workers' participation in the decision making process, he firmly believed that the management must solicit workers' consent on the issues and matters that concern them directly or even indirectly, since they also stake their fate in the success and failure of business. This is amply proved through his initiatives for mediation and arbitration in disputes of workers and mill-owners in Mumbai (Bombay) and Ahmedabad, the two industrial hubs of India. When he mediated between workers and managerial staff, he strongly held the view that both are complementary to each other, hence must work in collaboration and cooperation. Isolating workers from the decision making process is detrimental to the health of an organization, since their participation is a necessity for growth and development. Mill owners cannot benefit for long by creating a rift amongst them and by depriving them of their legitimate right to share the company's profit. Similarly, workers also cannot gain much in the long run by agitation, violence, strikes and disruption of work. Contemporary Indian corporates too have come to realise this truth and hence resort to necessary changes in their management policies.

The only unchangeable fact about the world is that it is constantly changing. Change is inevitable. Gandhi was well aware of the imperativeness of change with time and of the need to become responsive to the demands of changing conditions. He was resilient to change with 'change' but he was resolute not to change if change would mean to compromise the 'truth'. This has come out categorically in his following statement (7): "I must say what I feel and think at the moment [...] At the time of writing, I never think of what I said before. My aim is not to be consistent with my previous statement on a given question but to be consistent with truth as it may present itself to me at a given moment. The result is that I have grown from truth to truth." He further declares his readiness to embrace change based on emerging truth as his plumb line (8): "In my search after truth, I have discarded many ideas and learnt many new things."

SELF-MANAGEMENT

4

A question that often bugs the mind of many is why self-management and self-control are necessary. Why should they be a prerequisite to managing others? To elaborate this point, let us first glance through the following two statements, which are self- evidently true:

(i) A person unable to understand and analyse the self, and unable to exercise self-management, is invariably seen failing to appreciate the importance of the human factor in management. Precept not preaching, and action not acting, makes a real impact on the people's minds.

(ii) A thermodynamic function called entropy (physics/ chemistry) of a system is inversely related to the orderliness in the system, and it has a natural tendency to increase. What logically follows is that if a system were left to itself without any managing or controlling force, it would per se degenerate into a state of increasing randomness and disorderliness.

Therefore, to keep a system in order and to prevent it from

deteriorating, some force, tangible or intangible, internal or external, has got to be applied. A human being is like a super system that consists of various other systems: nervous, respiratory, circulatory or digestive. Though all these systems function independently, they are still required to work in symbiosis so as to keep the super system in an orderly and balanced state. Mind and body cannot be segregated from each other. The body's voluntary actions are subordinate to the state of mind which, in a common man, is easily affected by ambience. Hence, he could easily succumb to temptation, anger, frustration, revenge, lust and greed. If these negative forces are allowed to unleash and rule the mind, people often slip into a crisis, and society, into a catastrophe. But there is also an enlightened state of mind, called conscience, which is a highly ordered state endowed with justness and reasoning combined with kindness, sacrifice and compassion. This conscience is supremely able to apply checks and balances to the functioning of mind, and correspondingly to the body's activities and actions. A person who elevates himself/herself to this enlightened state is truly suited to managing self, and to managing and serving others.

In the case of human beings, moral or ethical deterioration directly related to the mental state, can occur if there are no controlling forces-internal or external – in whatever form. To maintain a standard level of moral and ethical values, one has to monitor oneself by applying checks and by taking corrective measures. If one's inner force is not enough to control and manage the self, and deviations from the ethical code of conduct become detrimental to the social matrix and human welfare, this code has got to be enforced or impressed upon via legislation.

Self-management is essentially an internal process of improving one's self towards the state of higher order in terms of mental, moral and ethical standards, and practice of it is rather incumbent on a person who has taken or has been entrusted with the responsibility of leadership. There are, among others, some specific tools of self-management such as self-introspection, self-actualisation, self-abnegation, self-repentance and self-confession.

Let me cite here from the experience of actor Ben Kingsley, who enacted Gandhi in Richard Attenborough's film 'Gandhi'. He played the character with great zest and finesse. Reportedly, he confessed to the media about his self-introspecting and conscious efforts for self-management before shooting of the film. To be able to give his best performance, he had lived for some time with Mahatma Gandhi in his psyche: he abjured alcohol, took to vegetarianism, controlled his passion, anger, jealousy and other temptations and aberrations. He confessed that after this period of self-control, his performance had been most satisfying to him and the viewers, which could otherwise not have been possible. An important cue that if self-management for a specific purpose, practiced for even a short period of time, can affect the state of mind and bring about an attitudinal transformation and push an individual to *summum bonum*.

One has to have control over oneself before even thinking of controlling or managing others. However, the difficulty in managing the self is created by our own misunderstood self-perception. We consider 'self' as a singular entity 'I'. While the fact is that the 'self' consists of two parts:

managing self and managed self. Segregation of the two from the apparently seamless one self, is heavily self-constrained, owing to one's own ignorance or arrogance and egocentricity. Individuals often have the tendency to attribute success to one's own ability, personality and efforts, and attribute failures to external factors such as lack of adequate means, a conducive environment, team spirit etc. This self-serving or self-aggrandising bias often becomes an impediment in the analysis and assessment of the self. But self-management without critical self-analysis is a futile exercise. The 'self-serving bias' has to be, therefore, neutralised by keeping transparency and being true to the self with unalloyed conscience. In many activities not warranted by the norms of any civilised and humane society, the 'self' may be tempted to make indulgence and is required to be managed by the 'managing self' which at this juncture, evokes conscience and controls the unrestrained thoughts swarming the mind. Depending on the magnitude of the inner force or voice of conscience, the 'managing self' regulates the behaviour of a person. Unless we recognise the importance of conscience and inner force, we shall either treat self-analysis — a precursor to self-management – as redundant, or shall continue to roam in the maze of self-management. For 'self-analysis', we need to examine ourselves critically and objectively. To understand right vs. wrong, we have to listen to the voice of our conscience – the voice of inner force. And for this to happen, there must be some moments of quietness devoted to non-partial self-intervention with a calm and cool mind. This is what meditation talks all about. Both self-management and meditation support each other, work in harmony and constitute the quintessential part of Gandhian management. Edward Thompson remarked very correctly about Gandhi, "Not since Socrates has world seen his equal for absolute self-control".

According to Maslow[1], self-realisation and actualisation (a state of creative evolution), can be achieved only after the satiation of various lower level needs – hunger, sex, shelter, security, self-esteem, in ascending order – which have a tendency to increase and linger on, unless kept under control. However, the need satisfying process may not necessarily go according to Maslow's hierarchy since a person can also work for satisfying his/her multiple needs at the same time.

According to Gandhi's views, one has to learn how to control and limit the desires which often turn into greed and constantly intensify, and have no definite boundary lines. Here comes the role of fasting to control hunger, of self-abnegation to control greed/Freudian Id (a component of personality identified by Sigmund Freud, the most influential figure in modern psychiatry) and of humility to control ego. On self-realization, worldly gratifications including money, work no more as motivators. When one comes out of the cocooned self and sees the world as one community and welfare of all as the ultimate goal, searching for truth, peace and harmony takes priority in the mind. It is the individual, after all, who constitutes a group; many such groups constitute a religious and social group; and many groups make a State. Thus, every individual is important in the making of a good society. That is why Gandhi addressed the issue of self-management as a primary requirement for character

---

1. Abraham Maslow - known for his theory of Hierarchy of Needs.

building of every individual and hence the character building of a nation.

Ruskin[2] had argued that the true wealth of a community lay in the well-being of all its members, and the good of an individual being contained in the good of all. If so, each individual has to learn first to be a good human being in order to participate in the building of a good society. This concept is reflected in the Gandhian viewpoint on *sarvodaya*. To realise the world as one fraternity and to understand the importance of good for all, is a complex subject and can be understood only by people of higher conscience. What differentiates a good and conscientious human being from the ones of lower instincts, close to an animal's, is this conscience. An animal learns to respond quickly if its lower level physical needs are satisfied. For instance, a rat learns faster to move across a maze if it finds food repetitively at the end of it. Even a virtual stimulus can elicit response from animals if a correspondence has been established earlier with the real stimulus. A dog starts salivating on the ringing of a bell if some positive correlation between this sound and the availability of desired food has been established in its mind. In all these situations, fulfillment of lower level needs works as a reminder and reinforcer. The reverse is also seen to be true, that is, the absence of a need satisfier would result in the withdrawal of response. This classical conditioning of stimulus-response (S-R) bond is largely effective in the animal world, though it can also be used as a technique to accelerate elementary learning process in children. S-R bonding has also been often found strong in

2. John Ruskin – a British arts and social critic, author of many books on architecture, social and industrial issues. His great book *'Unto the Last'* made a deep and lasting impression on Gandhi.

adults particularly of lower instincts, which make them an easy prey of greed, lust and other vices, hence most gullible in the hands of goons and susceptible to commit crimes of all sorts. The process of higher learning where both insight and intelligence matter does not get reinforced this way. Gestaltists argue that higher learning can be activated successfully with a holistic view or configuration of a subject or problem, which should be understood in its entirety and tackled in totality. But to understand the importance of values and good relationship between the self and the surrounding, and to realise the importance of duties and responsibilities against the claim for rights is a subject not only of higher learning but also of higher conscience and hence higher order management.

In the process of self-management, it is quite important that one learns to discard the crutches of dependence on others. And it is possible if one tries to become self-restraint and self-reliant for which one needs to have moral uprightness, intellectual self-assurance, emotional maturity and physical fitness, the latter two being necessary to endure stress and strain which any activity – physical or mental-invariably leaves behind. Although Gandhi was quite particular about the fitness of body, he was not a hypochondriac. He believed that due attention should be given to personal hygiene and nature-friendly methods for keeping oneself physically fit and mentally healthy.

Self-help, he believed, is the first training stage to prepare oneself for service to society. If we cannot perform our own work, how do we serve others? Various incidents speak a lot of his conscious and constant efforts towards self-service and self management:

During his sojourn with Sri Gokhale[3] in South Africa, he clipped his hair and washed his clothes, not because he couldn't afford the charges of a barber or a washer man, but because he didn't want to be helplessly dependent. The level of self-control and humility in him was further enhanced when he willingly cleaned toilets at colonies of lowly esteemed inhabitants.

Confession is an age-old method of self-introspection and self-management, which Gandhi appears to have practiced from childhood. At one instance when he was just a schoolboy, he pilfered a few coins from the pocket of his father's coat. But soon realising that this was an immoral act, he wept, repented and confessed.

Consuming alcoholic drinks and having extra-marital relationships may have been accepted as a part of life in the West and even in some so-called high societies in the East, but for Gandhi who, after his marriage, stayed in England in his young age, it was a test of self-determination and self-control where managing-self was to lead the managed-self. He unconditionally qualified it by refraining from the aforesaid intemperance, and thus fulfilling the vow given to his mother on the eve of his departure to England. Against his youthful age and influence of his local peer group, it was the manifestation of a very high degree of self-control and self-management.

Gandhi's emotional maturity perhaps reached a level where life and death were seen in continuum and were taken only as diminutive things against his values and principles. We

3. Gokhale, Gopal Krishna – an Indian scholar and academician who vigorously opposed recruiting of indentured labour in India.

can peep into this aspect through one critical incident in his life: In 1908, news of his wife's serious illness reached him while he was in jail. He could have managed to get himself released by paying the fine, and met his wife at the deathbed, but that would have been against his self-imposed code of conduct. Deeply saddened, he wrote a letter[4] to his wife in Gujarati: "I have received Mr Wests' telegram today about your illness. It cuts my heart [...] My coming there is out of the question. I can only come if I forgo *satyagrah* and pay a fine, which I must not."

---

4. *'Gandhi - A Life'*, Krishna Kriplani, p. 77, third reprint 1985, National Book Trust, New Delhi.

MANAGEMENT BY 'SAY-NO'

5

Abdication is as important as adoption. Just-in-time negation (JITNEG) is as crucial as on-time affirmation (OTA), and 'say-no' is an active mode of expression of disagreement. By some code of mannerism, say-no may be classified as a crude method of dissension or withdrawal, but it is an indicator of non-indulgence, independence, clarity, boldness and self-assurance. If you demur to say 'no' at the right time to what is being imposed upon you overtly or covertly against your conscience, you are partly or fully acquiescing in it. It requires courage and will to call a spade a spade, particularly when 'say-no' threatens the stability of a dominant system or undermines the superiority of a group, class or individual. However, 'say-no' need not be spoken always with crude gestures and rude utterances, or by making fatuous grimaces or grim faces.

Emotion-gushed 'no' or 'yes' is seldom sustained, hence slimly reliable; melodramatically or metaphorically effusing a mild 'yes' to regale, or mild 'no' to refuse something or somebody, is often misleading. Firm 'no' and firm 'yes' always derive strength from logically sound convictions and conventions; they stand on courage, sacrifice and confidence. In the Gandhian style, 'say-no' is combined with humility and firmness.

The passive method of saying 'no' is non-cooperation and, in the form of a movement, it is demonstrative of the collective 'no' of a group. As the gravity of some issues escalates, owing to the unilateral decisions and apathetic functioning of authorities, 'say-no' may also turn into a mass movement or civil disobedience, which calls upon the people to refrain from their normal day work to register their protest soberly and non-violently. Under acute conditions, fear is not misplaced if emotions get heightened and so erupt that the dissenters may resort to violence. Gandhian management by 'say-no' pleads for non-cooperation and civil disobedience as a means to ventilate escalated emotions pent up in people's minds, and let off the steam of their anger with maximum possible restraint and minimum possible damage. It may be surprising but is a fact that the greater the degree of calm while dissenting, the more is the suppressor shaken. And the greater the degree of sacrifice, the more is the oppressor baffled.

'Say-no' may not always be strategically or politically a correct proposition, as it can also harm one's own interest and personal material gains, but ethically it clarifies one's stand point, letting others choose their option and their own course of action. However, in order to gather self-confidence and render support to one's conscience in saying 'no' to others, one has to first learn at some point of time, to refuse one's own temptations, desires and anger. Reference is made here again to 'managing self' and 'managed-self' as discussed in Chapter IV, a prerequisite to managing others.

Some vignettes of Gandhi's life are reproduced below to look into his management style by saying 'no'.

He learnt saying 'no' to himself much before he entered into his profession, followed by his everlasting public interaction. On the eve of his departure (1888) from India to study law in England, he vouched for himself, as demanded also by his mother, to keep away from wine, meat and intimate relationships with any woman other than his wife. Gandhi wrote (1) in 'My Experiments With Truth' that he did stand by this word given to his mother, and we have reasons to believe it was true.

After completing his law studies in England, Gandhi started his practice in the Bombay courts. Soon, he defined a certain code of professional conduct for himself. For example, if the events connected with the case as narrated to him by his clients were ever found false and concocted, he would not continue with the suit further to plead for acquittal, relief, or compensation and would even cancel his contract saying 'no' to his client.

Gandhi's method of 'say-no' is also a peculiar combination of faith and logic, as seen in the following incident: Mr Coates was one of his Christian friends in Pretoria. Noticing one day a necklace of basil (tulsi) beads around Gandhi's neck, Coates ridiculed him for his superstition, and proposed to break the necklace. "No you will not break it; it is a sacred gift from my mother" interjected Gandhi. (2) Questioned by Coates about his belief in wearing such an article, Gandhi continued, "I do not think I should come to harm if I did not wear it, but I cannot without sufficient reason give up a necklace that she put around my neck out of love and in the conviction that it would be conducive to my welfare. When, with the passage of time, it wears away and breaks of its own, I shall have no desire to get a new one."

Before embarking upon a genuine bid to protect the rights of common men, one should desirably test one's own level of determination, courage and commitment to a cause. Already equipped with the knowledge of law, combined with tolerance and self-control, Gandhi began practicing 'say-no' first to protect his own rights. Later on, he undertook responsibility of public interest litigation (PIL) petitions and representations. When he grew morally bolder and managerially cleverer, he led many demonstrations, strikes, non-cooperation and civil disobedience movements. Two incidents quoted here indicate how he defended his legal rights and put utmost resistance to being coercively seized of his lawful possession:

Once in South Africa, Gandhi was to cover his journey by stagecoach from Charleston to Johannesburg. While contemptuously asked by the conductor to sit with the coachman on the box outside, the conductor himself sat inside with the English passengers. Gandhi bore this differential and insulting treatment just to avoid altercation which might have resulted in missing the coach altogether. On the way, the conductor wanted to smoke and therefore demanded Gandhi to vacate his seat. He scornfully asked him to sit on the footboard and give him space, which Gandhi didn't agree to. In a fit of anger, the conductor started punching on Gandhi, but still the latter refused to yield, didn't give up his right to be in the seat, and more importantly did not retaliate. On seeing the brutal behaviour of the conductor, white passengers protested, and the latter had to give Gandhi his seat. This was his strong 'no' to the wrong, defying even danger to his life.

An almost similar embarrassment Gandhi faced in a Durban court, where the Magistrate insisted that he take off his turban. He refused to comply and left. He wrote to the press about the incident, and the court's unfounded objection to his wearing an Indian turban — a sign of self-esteem.

However, in another incident, similar in nature and cause, that took place in the Supreme Court of Natal, Gandhi conceded to the order of the court and removed his turban. He felt slighted, but did not register his 'emphatic no'. Perhaps, his long stay in South Africa and his experience with the authorities made him mature both politically and strategically.

The moral authority in 'no' does not come from the arrogance of power and superiority of position but from simplicity, morality, sagacity, and veracity. In the biography 'The Life and Times of Mahatma Gandhi', author Robert Fischer said: "Power is the attribute of a machine; authority is the attribute of a person." And this was the difference between the 'say-no' of Winston Churchill and the 'say-no' of Gandhi. A relevant portion of Churchill's speech (3) in Parliament in reference to the dominion status of India reads: "In dealing with the oriental races... it is a mistake to try to gloss over grave differences, to try to dress up proposals in an unwarrantably favourable guise, to ignore or conceal or put in the background rugged but unpleasant facts. The right course on the contrary is to state soberly and firmly what the British position is, and not be afraid to say 'this would not suit us', ... 'There is no change of this coming to pass', 'We shall not agree to that being done. All these firm negatives ought to be told frankly and plainly." Here, Churchill is seen aggressively emphatic on 'management by say- no', but loaded with arrogance, power and contempt.

Unfortunately, the emissaries of England were holding often-unproductive parleys and discussions, taking pre-emptive decisions and making perforated assurances with folksy language in matters of vital importance for the people of India. This lowered the credibility of British authorities and forced even a person like Gandhi to say 'no' curtly to Stafford Cripps who, in 1942, came to New Delhi with a specific mission to discuss with Indian leaders a proposal for constitutional changes. The proposal had certain terms of Second World War time operations, and provisions of post-war settlements that were not in line with the apodictic principles and welfare policies of Gandhi, and by and large of the Congress too. After a summary discussion on the proposal in a meeting with Cripps, Gandhi rejected it circumspectly and expressed his negation allegorically in the following words (4): "Why did you come if this is what you have to offer? If this is your entire proposal to India, I would advise you to take the next plane home..."

MANAGEMENT BY EFFECTIVE COMMUNICATION AND INFORMATION FLOW

6

One most intriguing lesson to learn from the history of Gandhi's life is how he established a strong link with people of all rungs and strata, particularly the masses spread across the country including far-flung rural, hardly reachable-, and inhospitable areas, and how he managed to unite and mobilise them timely to follow his instructions and directions voluntarily. Regardless of the place from where he activated his programmes or launched his movements in the form of civil disobedience (*satyagrah*) and strike (*hartal*), his words moved people of all backgrounds.

Effective communication, which means a package of information, designed and delivered with proper content, method and channel, is vital to bringing about a directed change in the perception of the target group. Since information and perception are mutually interactive and interdependent, the alloyed information can distort the perception, while the distorted perception can alloy the information. The communication should, therefore, be made with caution and candour in order to impress a positive effect on the listener. Correspondingly, people contributing to the process of information flow, are required to have special traits, i.e. intellectual soundness, emotional maturity, unwavering tolerance and objective orientation. Otherwise, the information would lose its conformity with reality, and communication would deviate from its purpose.

Gandhi evoked people's right to freedom of communication with each other as a doctrine of natural justice, which is clear from his following statement[1]: "If the luxury of wires be denied to us, we must manage with the post. If the postal communication be also stopped, we must use messengers. Friends travelling to and from will oblige us. When the use of railways is denied, we must use other methods of conveyance. No amount of slowness imposed can checkmate us, if we are sure within." Any restriction imposed on the right to communicate freely, and right to access information would be tantamount to curtailing many other freedoms, including economic freedom which is contingent upon communication and access to relevant information.

George A. Akerlof, A. Michael Spence and Joseph E. Stiglitz, worked on the formulation of models[2] to explain how imbalances in information possession impact economic conditions, and they won the Nobel Prize in Economics for the year 2001. They proposed a common explanation in their analysis, with the realistic assumption

---

1. *The Collected Works of Mahatma Gandhi'*, Vol. 22 (Dec. 1921 – March 1922), Publication Division, Ministry of I & B, Government of India, New Delhi.

2. (a) http://www.nobel.se./economics/2001/public.html
   (b) http://www.berkeley.edu/news/features/2001/nobel

of asymmetric and askew information to answer many familiar but probing questions: Why are interest rates often excessively high on local lending markets in third world countries? Why do people who want to buy a good used car turn to a dealer rather than a private seller? Why does a firm pay dividends, even if they are taxed more heavily than capital gains? Why do rich land owners not bear the entire harvest risk in contracts with poor tenants?

Gandhi empowered common men by providing necessary inputs through oral communication and printed information dissemination, so as to enhance their awareness, augment their knowledge and raise their cognition level, all prerequisites to acquiring the ability to differentiate between right and wrong, identify threats and opportunities and recognise one's rights and responsibilities. For this, he thought it essential that the sources of information were reliable and access to these sources was open to all, not restricted to a select few. He also felt that an information-deficient person is not only indecisive, but also pliable and too easy to persuade. He, therefore, wanted the information-poor to be brought at par with the information-rich. If he were to witness the digital advances of the present time, he would have been deeply critical of the prevailing digital divide.

Gandhi used all methods and means of communication and information transmission. His communication – oral or written – was clear, concise and crisp, hence effective. He gave interviews, attended and addressed gatherings and meetings, wrote articles and travelled extensively to deliver his message all across the states of South Africa, India and the UK. And when or where he could not make his presence, he sent out notes, letters, appeals, warnings, greetings and condolences. His friends, followers and even critics and adversaries were his messengers. I feel for sure that if e-mail and sms were already invented in his era, he would have liked to use them vigorously, both in synchronous and asynchronous modes, but he would have still continued reaching the unreached to listen to their woes and agonies personally.

He issued in 1895 an appeal – *'To Every Briton in South Africa'*, highly acclaimed by the paper – *Natal Mercury* for its vividness and boldness. He also gave an account of the plight of Indians in South Africa in a series of articles written in 1899 for *The Times of India*. On the Natal Bill introducing poll tax, he wrote in April 1902 a special article again for *The Times of India* and urged the editor to raise his voice against injustice. Expressing deep concern over the conditions of Indians in Natal, he wrote, from Johannesburg, to the Indian National Congress held in 1903 in Madras (now Chennai), India.

Gandhi's interaction, both lateral and vertical, with different classes of people having diverse backgrounds, convinced him that the masses have great potential to effect social change and renaissance. He also knew well that both language and semantics could be at times a strong barrier to communication. Hence, for harnessing the potential of common men in expediting the process of change, he thought it imperative to communicate with them in their own language, in which they could comfortably express views and understand issues.

On matters of social, political, legal and economic importance, he would often make references and have discussions first in public and then take them up for debate with the government. It was strategically important that information dispersal was made not only in English but also in many more languages, widely read and spoken by different linguistic segments of immigrants in South Africa and different communities in India. He realised the need of setting up some steady channels of communication and turned to print media, undertaking the responsibility for the publication of many daily, bi-weekly, weekly or monthly publications not only in English, but also in Hindi, Gujarati and Tamil.

Newspaper publication is a job of great responsibility and has to be done assiduously, as it does not only end with receiving information and reproducing it to readers, but also calls for unbiased interpretation, verification, accurate translation if required, of this information, and its timely publication and circulation. Gandhi launched the weekly paper *Indian Opinion* in 1904 in South Aftica. It was published from Durban in four languages – English, Hindi, Gujarati and Tamil. Not only Gandhi did finance the paper, but also took up the entire burden of its publication, and wrote editorials and special technical articles for it. The existence of *Indian Opinion* contributed to the success of *satyagrah* that he experimented for the first time in South Africa. This journal remained his primary instrument in the struggle for all time to come.

An English bi-weekly, *Young India* was started under his supervision in 1919, from Bombay. The galaxy of luminaries who contributed, included C.F.Andrews, Mahadev Desai, C. Rajagopalachari, George Joseph and Tagore. The Jallianawallah Bagh episode was published, which also gave reportage on the miserable conditions of farmers and labourers.

Navjivan, a Gujarati monthly published under his supervision, narrated the problems of mill owners and workers,
bringing out his appeal to both working in harmony and
mutual trust. He stressed that workers must strive for the
increase in production, and owners must take measures to
better the life of workers.

Rapid changes in the field of communication and
information technologies in developed countries have
made them information bankers and, at times, brokers too.
They can swarm underdeveloped and developing countries
with all sorts of biased opinions and lopsided information,
sometimes with a specific intent to polarise the audience.
UNESCO's MacBridge Commission[3] recognised the
importance of information flow for cultural, social and
economic development, hence proposed a new World
Information Communication Order (NWICO) as a means
of correcting imbalances and inequalities created by one-
way free flow of information. The Commission stated:
"There can be no genuine, effective independence without
the communication resources needed to safeguard it".
NWICO made provision for all nations to be granted the
right to communicate and access information, hence the
opportunity to share air-waves and air-time equitably on
communication satellites.

Channels of communication in British India were
invariably throttled or blocked, and authorities often
worked on supposition and suspicion and responded with
indifference. The information flow was practically
unidirectional. British censorship succeeded in blocking
publication of reports on the Jallianwala Bagh (Amritsar)

---

3. Macbridge Commission - 'Many Voices, One World', UNESCO, Paris, 1980.

massacre of April 1919. The Administration spoke of
these events only evasively and censored material information reaching even the United States – the country which
was genuinely concerned then with the freedom of press
and political developments in India. Against limited means
of communication, against possible threat of information
suppression, and against severely restricted freedom of
speech, Gandhi achieved amazing success in communicating with people across the globe. Just imagine if television
and Internet were also available in his time, the reach and
impact of his communication would have been a mind-
boggling phenomenon. That is why in this age of hi-tech
communication, his name has been chosen, nearly sixty
years after his death, as the brand ambassador 'Apple
Gandhi' for Apple Macintosh and as 'Telecom Italia
Gandhi' for Telecom Italia.

While Gandhi preferred a federal approach to information
management by granting full freedom to press and to an
individual, group or organisation for the acquisition,
storage and dissemination of information, he held the
press wholly accountable in discharging its duties
prudently and responsibly to meet societal obligations.
Lapsus calami (a slip of the pen) on the part of an editor
or reporter, can distort the message so much, that it can
cause irreversible damage to a system and society, which
could be as disastrous as *lapsus linguae* (a slip of the
tongue) on the part of any religious or political leader or
country's head. Once he observed[4]: "I realised that the sole
aim of journalism should be service. The press is great
power, but just as an unchanged torrent of water

---

4. *Indian Opinion*, 3 June, 1903

submerges a whole countryside and devastates crops even so an uncontrolled pen serves but to destroy. If the control is from without, it proves more poisonous than want of control. It can be profitable only when exercised from within."

To increase their audiences and attract sponsorship, the management of many print and electronic media resort to unethical and unsavoury practices. For 'increase of sale' and 'product promotion', companies and advertising agencies have made a nexus with the managements of both print and electronic media. They reserve premium space in magazines and newspapers, and buy premium time on TV and radio channels, to attack a very large audience with vigorous ad campaigns, often filled with lewd audios, visuals, graphics and clippings. Even the management of leading newspapers and magazines of good and long standing do the same. They justify their irresponsible and condemnable act in the name of freedom of press and 'promotion of aesthetics and commercial art', thus glorifying themselves as saviour of the people's right to freedom of expression and access to information. But such messages impact the minds of young readers, corrupt their thoughts and actions, and eventually vitiate and criminalise society. Gandhi reiterates these ideas in the following[5]:

"No country and no language are free from obscene literature. As long as there are self-indulging and immoral people in the world, obscene literature will continue to be produced and read. But when such literature is disseminated through newspapers of good standing, under the guise

---

5. *Navjivan* (Hindi), 6 March 1930.

of art or service, it is truly horrible... to publish such
things in the name of reform is unnecessary and harmful
[...] Its readership can only be of two types: the educated
debauch who wish to satisfy their lust by any means, and
innocent men who, though so far free from the ways of
vice, are so impressionable that they may be corrupted. For
such people obscene literature is fatal."

It is difficult to guess whether any legislation can strictly
check the publication of obscene material even in widely
circulated and popular magazines and newspapers, but it is
heartening to read clause 67, chapter XI, of IT ACT 2000,
GOI, on publishing of information which is obscene in
electronic form:

"Whoever publishes or transmits or causes to be published
in the electronic form, any material which is lascivious or
appeals to the prurient interest or its effect is such as to
deprave and corrupt the persons who are likely, having
regard to all relevant circumstances, to read, see or hear the
matter contained or embodied in it, shall be punished on
first conviction with imprisonment of either description
for a term which may extend to five years and with fine
which may extend to one lac (hundred thousand) rupees,
and in the event of a second or subsequent conviction with
imprison-ment of either description ten years and also
with fine which may extend to two lacs of rupees."

As regards the usage of different channels of communication, he used upward channel to submit his appeals,
petitions and requests to authorities, and also to persuade
his seniors to his viewpoint. Since he never regarded
himself as superior to any human being, he considered it
improper to issue instructions as a caveat or whip in the

downward channel. He often advised people not to act under duress or physical or mental coercion. If they were to act according to what he said, they were to do it under their free will. In horizontal communication at peer level, Gandhi maintained his cool as a patient listener and his nobility as a tolerant organiser. He made regular consultations with the members of his groups and seriously pondered over their suggestions and comments, and never hastened to take decision a priori or presumptuously on issues of public interest, and national or international importance. His associates were also working as distributaries and tributaries of his message to every corner of the country. Amazingly, this grapevine channel through which flowed his message continually, never distorted any information, on or from him, carried forward from one node to another. A remarkable quality of Gandhi was that irrespective of his busy schedules and meetings, he used to ascertain the situation and assess the problems himself, in addition to gleaning information from media, travellers and his emissaries.

Observing silence is also a medium of communicating messages, meanings and feelings. This was first demonstrated by Gandhi. His silence conveyed a specific meaning that was no less effective than words from his mouth. His muteness sent equally vibrant ripples as his oral communication.

Another medium he often used for registering his compunction or disapproval, was taking recourse to fasting. For any slip on his part or any wrong committed by his fellow-beings or followers, he made confession and expressed his repentance and remorse by holding silence or observing a fast. "For confession of errors," Gandhi wrote explicitly, "is like a broom that sweeps away dirt and leaves the surface cleaner and brighter [...] I shall continue to confess blunders each time the people commit them.............."

Gandhi succeeded in reaching close to the people by combating all barriers to communication viz. language, distance, ego, perception, motive and hierarchy. Even the most sequestered and deprived communities of that time were netted close to him since they felt blessed and protected beside him.

Attiring in a particular form and style adds to the overall message. Dressing up in accordance with a given protocol may be desirable and may suit to an occasion, but it can also disguise the brute for a civilized one and the scoundrel for a sage. Gandhi's scanty clothes on his body that remained only half-covered, spoke of a body language (kinesics), which identified him with the stark poverty of roadside slum dwellers and tillers in the fields, shivering in winter and sweating in summer. Attired the way many millions in the world far below poverty line do, he not only established his identity as one of them, but also made his communication direct and full of impact.

Use of short comments without superfluous phrases and redundant words was the hallmark of his effective communication. With economy of words, his messages contained soul-searching questions and heart-winning answers. Though stoic and steadfast, Gandhi could still decipher the language of rolling tears and decrypt the meanings of broken words. Hearing one day some criticism against one of his mentors, Dadabhai Naoroji, who gave away a substantial part of his wealth to the needy poor and for the cause of India's struggle for freedom, Gandhi went to him and expressed his concern with doubts. Dadabhai spoke to him poignantly: "What reply do I give you? Do you believe these things?" Noting anguish in these words, tears welled in Gandhi's eyes and he immediately regretted[6] and said: "I do not want to hear anything more. I have no trace of doubt left in me."

A leader or a ruler must have, in addition to oft-quoted attributes of leadership, sensitivity and sensibility. Only then can he or she dedicate a life truly to the service of the people. According to a Korean parable[7], crown prince T'ai was asked by his father to spend some time before the coronation ceremony in the company of temple master Pan Ku, for garnering more knowledge and acquiring more wisdom After many days of routine discourse, the temple master explained to the prince, at the time of his departure, the qualities of a true ruler: "To hear the unheard is a necessary discipline to be a good ruler. For only when a ruler has learned to listen closely to the people's heart – hearing their feelings un-communicated, pains unexpressed and complaints unspoken – can he hope to inspire confidence in his people, understand when something is wrong, and can feel the true needs of his citizens."

Gandhi was not a ruler but as a superb leader, he ruled the hearts and minds of millions of people in this world.

---

6. *Navjivan* (Gujarati), 7 September 1924.
7. Harvard Business Review, July-Aug 1992, p-123, 'Parables of Leadership' by Chan Kim and Renee A. Mouborgn.

MANAGEMENT BY PRINCIPLES OF
NATURAL JUSTICE

7

"The symbol of a court of Justice is a pair of scales held evenly by an impartial and blind but sagacious woman. Fate has purposely made her blind in order that she may not judge a person from his exterior but from his intrinsic worth."
—Mahatma Gandhi

*

The purpose of framing laws and enforcing them in any system, society or organisation, is to set an order in it so that the guilty and errant are punished and the innocent are protected and compensated for losses suffered. According to the principle of natural justice, a person has also to be given a fair opportunity to speak and defend him or herself against allegations and charges leveled. The result, however, depends purely on the court's standpoint and judgment (both being contingent upon the interpretation of law), the perception of judges, authenticity of evidence and presentation of witnesses. But proceedings before a judge in any court of law are aimed at investigating the truth.

Inherent limitation in most proceedings of the court is the uncertainty in properly retrieving all necessary, authentic documents and evidence related to the case or event of the past when none of the judges deciding the case was actually present at the time and place of its occurrence. If the proceedings of a case drag on for too long, it leaves enough room for human error, tampering of evidence, wear and tear of files or CDs, biasing of witnesses and judicial inconsistency. Consequently, many interrelated factors playing a crucial role in configuring the truth may remain incomprehensible, incomplete and obscure. The situation may get further worsened to if the judiciary does not keep restraint and become vulnerable to purse, pressure, prejudices and preferences. Why should not then the judiciary be also made transparent and accountable?

Gandhi wrote in his autobiography[1]: "As a student, I heard that the lawyer's profession was a liar's profession, but this did not influence me as I had no intention of earning either position or money by lying." Gandhi's reluctance to pursue his legal profession actively in courts was a reflection of his anguish over what he saw there: that fame and material success of an attorney during at least the initial years of his career depended mostly on unethical practices like paying touts, commission to other lawyers, extorting money even from the poor, proving wrong as right, and at times degrading one's self-esteem before the court. His conscience did not permit him to tread the trodden path. He once said[2]: "I learnt that the true

---

1. 'An Autobiography' by M. K. Gandhi (Translated from Gujarati by Mahadeo Desai) p.302, Ch. XLIV, Part IV, 1980 Navjivan Publishing House, Ahmedabad.

2. Ibid. p.112, Ch.XIV, Part II

function of a lawyer is to unite parties rivet asunder" and that he proved by settling a majority of cases outside the court. The case of Abdullah & Co, for which he was engaged as an attorney on long term basis, and set out his first voyage to Durban (South Africa), was finally settled by him outside the court. He was convinced that the settlement of a dispute by mediation, reconciliation and/or arbitration outside the jurisdiction of court is less time consuming, less hassle ridden, less expensive for both parties and less burdensome to the one liable to pay compensation. He believed in the goodness of man, hence despised crime, not the criminal, and disdained sin, not the sinner.

It is most commonly observed that an attorney supposed to investigate and uphold the truth above all, interprets a 'matter of legality' very often at the expense of 'matter of reality (truth)'. Acts and Statutes quoted in the proceedings of a court are often truncated and twisted by a lawyer to suit the requirement of the petitioner or respondent for winning the case. In this process, the lawyer often fails to observe ethics in legal practice.

A special feature of Gandhi's persona as a lawyer was not only his capability to understand the nuances and ramifications of any law or Act, but also his courage to counter it publicly in case the same was found con-travening the principles of humanity and natural justice. He considered the judiciary primarily an instrument to assess the truth and law as a weapon to protect it. But if the law itself provides avenues to silence truth and stifle humanity, there is something fundamentally wrong in the framing and promulgation of the law, since all that is legal may not be just – he believed. He often moved courts and appealed to authorities for amending those laws, repealing Acts and reviewing or withdrawing bills and ordinances found grossly inconsistent with the spirit of natural justice, incongruent with the canons of humanity and incompatible with the functioning of a welfare state. And if he could not succeed, he did not hesitate in mobilising people to rise from slumber and defy the enforcement of such repressive and coercive laws.

He used to attach as much importance to the *obiter dicta* of a court or government as to the *ratio decidendi*. In reference to the Transvaal Asiatic Registration Act (TARA) requiring compulsory registration of Indians by finger impression, Gandhi[3] said: "I think experience has made me something of an expert about laws. As I read this outrageous law, my hair stood on end and I felt there was something wrong about it. The law was so drafted as to make slave of us." The statement brings out a scholastic facet of Gandhi – the ever growing insight to examine law in the light of its legal implications and far reaching consequences.

Gandhi applied his expertise to framing of welfare and social policies and programmes which would guarantee fundamental rights and natural justice to all, particularly the people of weaker sections whose voice often went unheard. This was an important dimension of his managerial prowess that also embraced the development of untapped and grossly ignored section of human capital of the society. Unfortunately his stand taken added provoked the irritation of state authorities. And often placed him in a situation of confrontation with the government who

---

3. *Indian Opinion*, 29 Feb 1908.

branded him a 'political captor' and a 'social agitator'. He also subscribed to the view that legislation alone cannot bring about exaltation in society; and that human values and ethics are required to be nurtured in the code of conduct of every citizen. In a letter to *The Times of India* he wrote that[4] "prejudices cannot be removed by legislation [...] They will yield only to patient toil and education."

While dealing with litigations in courts, Gandhi always checked that all procedures were legally correct, that the legalese of the pact or offer was sound, and that details were placed before the competent authority at the right time. He followed just and lawful methods of protest such as appeal, petition and notice in the constitutional frame. When all these options failed, only then he resorted to *satyagrah*, regulated under his moral code of conduct. When in 1896 he planned a short trip to India, Indian immigrants of Natal (South Africa) persuaded him to convey their problems and grievances to the people of India. He acceded to their request and undertook the task of drafting and distributing the *Green Pamphlet* (named after the colour of its cover), containing a detailed account of their grievances. But to be legally correct and establish his identity as a spokesperson of the said group, he first sought their authorisation in a certificate, signed by the prominent citizens of Natal.

Deeply hurt by the humiliation of Indians in South Africa (SA), Gandhi organised large scale campaigns in the form of civil disobedience against the government on many counts: levying yearly tax of 3 pounds on the ex-

---

4. *The Times of India*, 2 June, 1918.

indentured labourers refusing to return to India; imposing ban on Asiatic immigrants in Transvaal; Cape Colony Supreme Court's order to recognise only Christian marriages.

Gandhi took up these issues again in his second meeting with General Smuts, who could see perhaps this time around, the purity in purpose and humility of the appeal. Hence, he submitted the Indian Relief Bill with a positive recommenda-tion to the Parliament of Capetown. The Bill was passed by Parliament and became an African Law which declared (i) the abolition of the 3 pounds tax on ex-indentured labourer; (ii) the discontinuance of the practice of drawing indentured labourers from India; and (iii) the validation of Indian marriages.

In another instance when Natal Legislature[5] was to discuss a Bill which contained a proposal to disenfranchise Indian immigrants, Gandhi expressed his resentment. He firmly believed that depriving people of a particular community after their settlement on a particular territory, of their right to vote, was not only unjust, but also a blatant humiliation. He telegraphed a request to the speaker of the Legislature for the postponement of the debate on this Bill until the Indians could be heard. Thereafter, he drafted a petition and posted its copies to the Legislature and the press. The petition came up for discussion, but only notionally, and the Bill was ultimately passed. This, however, did not deter him and he arranged to affix with the petition a list of as many signatures as possible, and sent it to Colonial Secretary in London. *The Times of India* in Bombay was kept informed of the development,

---

5. *The Life of Mahatma Gandhi'* by Louis Fischer, p.63, Harper Collins Publisher 2000, New Delhi.

and reported the matter as a precipitate of racial discrimination policy of the government. England did not
relish such negative publicity against its image of a
civilised nation, hence issued a directive to Natal
Legislature to amend the Bill (1897) that eventually came
out as the Natal Act[6], which annulled racial discrimination
but required immigrants to qualify through only an
educational test, thus giving them equal electoral right.
Gandhi's goal was achieved in principle of legality.

In India, his *satyagrah* movement was carried out on an
experimental basis for the first time in 1917, in
connection with the problems of indigo sharecroppers in
the Champaran district of the State of Bihar. These tenant
peasants were contracted by landlords so as to surrender
indigo harvest grown in 15 per cent of their holdings.
When the rainfall was scanty and the production low,
peasants faced hard times. In order to instill courage and
confidence in them to resist this imposed serfdom and
fight it out in court, Gandhi discovered his own methods:
he and his followers started working there not only as
councilors, pursuing and preparing them for a legal battle,
but also offered their services as sweepers and scavengers
to even out all the barriers of class, caste and creed. Gone
weary of Gandhi's strategic planning, a notice from the
local district authority, directing him to leave town, was
served. On his refusal to comply with it, he was summoned
to court on the following day. News of this spread like a
flash and thousands of peasants free from fear of their
landlords and from the fear of losing even their livelihood,
gathered at the court to prevent his arrest. Scared and

---

6. Ibid. p. 73.

baffled, the court released him immediately. The government set up an enquiry commission involving Gandhi as its member. In its report, it submitted a recommendation in favour of tenant farmers. As a result, the system to surrender a part of indigo cultivation to landlords was abolished. One may also recall here the famous Dandi March of 1930, defying the salt law and seeking natural justice for the common man.

Not only the applied knowledge of law was Gandhi's forte, but it was also his sensitive cognition. He often read between the lines and sensed impending danger. The Rowlatt Report that introduced wartime measures in peaceful times, like suppression of freedom to public speech, suppression of the press and suppression of the right to assemble, made Gandhi restless. He could feel in between the lines a shadow of calamitous days ahead. The Legislative Council passed the report in early 1919. Gandhi[7] called it a "farce of legal formality" and publicly appealed to Viceroy Proselyte to withhold his approval. But the Viceroy ignored his request and signed it on March 18, 1919. The Rowlatt Act became a law less than four weeks from the carnage of Jallianawala Bagh (Amritsar, India), which took place on 13 April 1919. General R.E.H Dyer ordered open fire on thousands of innocents and unarmed public, without any provocation from their end, assembled for a meeting in an open ground, the so called Bagh (garden) in Amritsar. Who gave him the permission to shoot and kill is a question that has haunted history ever since. Two possibilities seem to emerge: one, that he got prior sanction from top advisors

---

7. *Mahatma Gandhi - A Great Life in Brief'* by Vincent Sheean, p.95, Publication Division, Ministry of I & B Government of India, 1982.

of the British Crown; and two, he overstepped his own authority. The first possibility is ruled out on the ground that top advisors couldn't have been politically so immature as to accord such an insane act. The second possibility, however, survives, as it appears to be rooted in the Rowlatt Act. General Dyer, an officer of long standing, would have never behaved so callously and inhumanly to stake his career, which was at its zenith, had he not thought of the Rowlatt Act as a shield to save him from criticism and as a legal instrument to protect him from impeachment. The Jallianwala Bagh massacre made Gandhi do a sharp U-turn and decide to use his super-managerial power as a political juggernaut.

ETHICS IN STRATEGIC MANAGEMENT

8

"In a great war, one strategy after another is adopted and abandoned. The aim behind all is one and the same. It is sometimes necessary to abandon a strategy as it may have been to adopt it"
—Mahatma Gandhi

*

The Oxford encyclopedia traces the origin of 'strategy' to the Latin word 'stratagem', which means maneuvering to achieve a goal or a plan to outwit opponents, especially in warfare and war-like operations. Its scope conventionally and clandestinely transgresses the ambit of all rules, norms and code of conduct.

Military hierarchies and imperialistic power world over have been built by nurturing deception, secretiveness and violence as the fundamental tenet of strategy, and by using wile and guile as its necessary components. The only imperative of the game is Rafferty's rule – no rules at all! But matter of concern is that if deception and surreptitiousness continue to receive acceptability and find applicability in national or international politics, treaties and agreements, rogues and rogue nations will rule the world. This may also ultimately lead to a breach of trust and faith in the comity of nations as also in religious and social groups, eventually frustrating all efforts of the UN for world peace and sustainable development.

Several events in the course of world history suggest that ethicality and strategy are poles apart. Strategic Defense Initiatives (SDI) in the past, advanced by the USA and Strategic Military Installations (SMI) made by erstwhile USSR, had originated from the mutual distrust between the two nations. Strategic entry of the East India company into the Indian peninsula and stealthy pacts of Adolf Hitler in World War II are indicators of ulterior motives and unethical bids for conquest and expansion of the empire. One is, therefore, led to believe that it is naivety, stupidity and unsound to talk of ethicality in strategy, for the two have different QWERTY and cannot be connected to each other. Likewise, in the corporate world, managers do avoid speaking on ethical practices, if any, in their business operations and managerial decisions aimed at only to multiplying profit and overriding competitors. It is commonly believed that business with ethical practices cannot yield their desired profit margin. Paradoxically, Gandhi argued to the contrary. His initiatives to settle disputes between mill owners and workers, and the major sustainable outcomes of his persuasion with the British authorities, bear ample evidence to this fact.

Gandhi was basically a strategist. But his perspective on strategic management was different altogether. His strategic moves were ethical and transparent, in sharp contrast with the prevalent meaning of the word. Humanistic elements and moral courage added intrinsic values to his approach, but most importantly, he intro- duced ethics into strategy. Polak quotes[1] Gandhi as having said in South Africa: "Men say I am a saint losing myself in politics. The fact is that I am a politician trying my hardest to be a saint."

Why can't a strategy be transparent and operative within the ethical norms, and still have the potential to outwit and subdue a competitor? In a game of chess, each move by a player is quite open and within the set rules and standards. Nothing is concealed, and it is up to the other player to guess the implications of the move forwarded by the first. In fact, the opponent's 'move' – could mean 'checkmate' or a forerunner to 'checkmate'. When it indicates check, the opponent is free to either reverse the move or put a defense or escape. There is no mention in the biographies or autobiography of Gandhi that he had ever played chess or showed interest in the game. However, his plans, including countrywide *satyagrah* were as if executed by an ace chess player.

Gandhi's strategy has the following characteristics:

(i) It is candid and transparent.

(ii) A common factor in all his strategic operations is ethicality.

(iii) 'What I say is what I do' (WISIWID).

(iv) Disagreement on contentious issues is communicated to the opponent in advance.

---

1. *The Life of Mahatma Gandhi*' by Louis Fischer, p.134, Harper collins Publisher India Pvt. Ltd. yr. 2000.

(v) Beliefs and assumptions have to pass a test of logic and reason.

(vi) Vigorous campaigns or drives against wrong do not mean violence.

(vii) Adopting or abandoning a policy or move in the light of a new truth is admissible well within the scope of ethicality.

Gandhi's epical Dandi march was obviously a bold and strategic move, but ethical too, because it had a humanitarian cause and was transparent to his adversaries. Truth, transparency, humility and firmness are found amazingly blended in his strategic ultimatum[2] given in this context to the government (via his letter dated March 2, 1930 written to the Viceroy) in clear terms: "On the 11th day of this month, I shall proceed with such co-workers as I take, to disregard the provisions of Salt Law [...] it is, I know, open to you to frustrate my design by arresting me."

Imposing a ban on the manufacturing and selling of salt, which is a basic ingredient for the common man, was sure to boomerang and Gandhi knew it very well. His simple and transparent strategy was first to remind lawmakers of their folly and lack of common sense in attacking the fundamental right to livelihood, and appeal to their conscience if they could revoke the law. In case he failed to get it revoked or amended, he would fire up the conscience of common men to rise against this law, and burden the British Administration with a sense of albatross guilt, thus making the law ultimately ineffectual.

---

2. *'Mahatma Gandhi – A Great Life in Brief'* by Vincent Sheean,p.133, Third Reprint 1982, Publication Division Ministry of Information & Broadcasting GOI, New Delhi.

To pick up a handful of salt from the seacoast, he walked an unusually long distance, not just to surprise, but also give enough time to the authorities to review their decision, gain time to propagate this news to every corner of the country, and allow anxious people to follow him and gather all along his route.

Gandhi's activities during India's struggle for freedom were already a centre of attraction for people in the country and abroad, and his name had become a mammoth crowd puller. However, he chose to start action strategically, from an appropriate location and an opportune time, so that his admirers and followers could assemble conveniently and a crowd could gather easily. He was well aware of the strategic importance of crowds, as it appears from his article 'Mass Action', containing an extract[3] from another article by Sir Martin Conway: "A crowd that has never come physically together gains greatly in vigour if it can be in whole or even in part embodied [...] An even more rudimentary application of the principle of crowd – attractiveness – is the organisation of procession. The longer they can be made, the more useful they are, and the more they attract and impose upon the outside."

For a successful outcome, a high level strategy has to be combined with high level commitment of the people involved. An impulsive move of a leader cannot be part of any planned strategy. Gandhi executed his plans only after he had analysed the environment, collected full information and found all related factors in place and under control. About the launch of his civil disobedience

---

3. 'Mass Action', an Article in Young India, 24 April 1930

campaign in Bardoli, then in Bombay, Gandhi had already written[4] to Lord Reading on February 1, 1922. But as clashes took place between the irate mob and repressive police force on February 5 in Chauri-Chaura district of U.P. (the then United Province), he did not hesitate to withdraw his plan, and suspended the campaign sine die, since he noticed the building-up of tension and people's proclivity to non-violence which he thought as a major hindrance to his strategy implementation. The suspension dampened the torrent of emotions and the degree of enthusiasm in the public. Gandhi, like any other strategist, knew fully well that without respecting and sustaining people's emotions and winning their confidence, no action plan could work. Therefore, for sustaining their high spirit and restoring their confidence, he interpreted his strategy openly[5]: "In a Great War, one strategy after another is adopted and abandoned. The aim behind all is one and the same. It is sometimes as necessary to abandon a strategy as it may have been to adopt it." Being an avowed lover of non-violence and staunch believer in peace, it may be noted that Gandhi did not always abhor violence as seen here[6]: "Where there is a choice between cowardice and violence, I advise violence [...] I would risk violence a thousand times rather than emasculation of the race [...] But I believe that non-violence is infinitely superior to violence; forgiveness is more manly than punishment." Such was his

4. Op. cit., 'Mahatma Gandhi - A Great Life in Brief', p. 113

5. 'Test for Ahmedabad and Surat' in 'The Collected Works of Mahatma Gandhi', p.4 71, Vol. 22 (Dec. 1921- March 1922), Publication Division, Ministry of Information & Broadcasting, GOI, New Delhi.

6. 'Mahatma Gandhi' by Romain Rolland (Translated from French by Catherine D. Groth) Reprinted with the permission of George Allen and Unwin Ltd. London, 1968; fourth impression pp.33-34, 1990, Publication Division, GOI, New Delhi.

appeal in simple terms that it moved the minds and hearts
of both people who had muscle power and people endowed
with analytical thinking.

Even though the truth was a guiding torch throughout his
life, he did not mind changing his previous stand or
strategy whenever he discovered a new truth in relation to
the present. Once he made a disclosure[7]: "My aim is not to
be consistent with my previous statement on a given
question, but to be consistent with truth as it may present
itself to me at a given moment. "During the World War-II,
England wanted Indians to join up with them and Indian
troops to work for them, but Indian Congress Party at this
juncture issued a resolution urging the British to leave
India, stating that only free democratic India like other
allies would resist Japanese advances. Wavell, successor of
Viceroy Linlithgow, wrote to Gandhi sarcastically in a
letter[8] dated 28th March 1944: "But you are much too
intelligent a man, Mr Gandhi, not to have realised that the
effect of your resolution must be to hamper the
prosecution of war and it is clear to me that you had lost
confidence in our ability to defend India [...], and were
prepared to take advantage of our supposed military straits
to gain political advantage." It was, however, not known to
Wavell that the resolution was drafted by other leaders and
was not inspired by Gandhi. Conscientiously unwilling to
make capital gain out of the crisis of an adversary, Gandhi
could have withheld or withdrawn the resolution, but he
didn't do so and contrastingly he neither made any

---

7. 'The life of Mahatma Gandhi' by Louis Fischer, p.440, Harper Collins Publisher
                                                                        Pvt, Ltd. yr, 2000.

8. 'Mahatma Gandhi and J.L. Nehru: A Historic Partnership', p.13 , Vol. III, by
     Madhu Limaye ,B .R. Publication Corp. 1990, New Delhi.

comment nor showed any reservation.

It was this virtual silence, which was taken as a signal of his concurrence. Perhaps, he was searching for an ethical justification in his strategic reticence against the void exercise that Cripps had made in his failed mission.

It is typical of Gandhi's strategy that any inhuman act of the adversary should be so exposed as to have it written on the wall. And the plain truth about his strategic planning was that it would counter the despotic moves and illicit plans of opponents even at the risk of his life. While leaving Bombay for Durban on his second trip to South Africa (SA), he was warned by one of his well-wishers that he had to guard himself against possible assault upon his arrival, schemed by some angry group of people prepared to forcibly deport him to India. This imbroglio was supposedly created by a 'misquoted' report, in a Durban newspaper, on the content and intent of the *Green Pamphlet* circulated by him in Bombay (now Mumbai). However, the pamphlet[9] contained only an appeal to the people of India to ponder seriously over the plight of Indians in South Africa. He did not change his programme and landed in Durban as per schedule. As expected, he was assaulted by a frenzied white mob. It was only due to the intervention of a white police official's wife that his life was saved. However, the shocking and brutal act of the assailants under the connivance of local authorities came to be known in different parts of the globe without any efforts from him, and millions became his sympathizers.

---

9. *'Mahatma Gandhi - A Chronology'* – compiled by K.P. Goswami, Publication Division, Ministry of Information and Broadcasting, GOI, 1971. The *Green Pamphlet* – as it is called – had a green cover and was published in 1896.

Resorting to fasts for too long on certain occasions, to the point of endangering his life, had a very specific purpose. While under house arrest in Agha Khan's palace in Poona, he began on February 9, 1943 his fast unto death. There was an acute difference of opinion between Churchill's Cabinet and Viceroy Linlithgow's Executive Council over the release of Gandhi. The government was to choose one out of the two options: (a) let Gandhi fast to death or (b) release him in view of possible danger to his life. Though Churchill was opposed to releasing him even during his fast, the Viceroy felt strongly about setting him free. Perhaps owing to his long experience and being directly in touch with the situation, Linlithgow's opinion prevailed and the government finally decided to release Gandhi. When Gandhi was informed, he deflected the offer finding it incompatible with the situation he was in as stated in his reply to the authorities[10]: "The impending fast has not been conceived to be taken as a free man [...] If, therefore, I am released, there will be no fast in terms of correspondence above mentioned. I shall have to survey the situation de novo and decide what I should do." Possibly, he did not find any positive correlation between the cause and consequence if he was released and still undertook the fast. Or he might have thought that undertaking the fast for a particular cause when free would not make the desired impact.

Whereas he had faith in the strength of masses, Gandhi also drew upon the intelligentsia. He, therefore, availed possibly all opportunities to visit premier educational institutions like the Banaras Hindu University, Aligarh

---

10. '*The Transfer of Power*' Madhu Limaye, pp841-843, Vol. IV B.R. Publication Corp. 1990, New Delhi.

Muslim University, Ahmedabad Vidyapith etc. in India, and Oxford, Cambridge and Eton in England. There, he enjoyed face-to-face interactions with the educated class and attempted to convince them of his value-based strategy and solicit their collaboration in the negotiation and execution of his plans. His strategic and bold proclamation[11] to continue India's cordial relationship with England has been a subject of study for academics, foreign policy makers and political analysts : "I would cut India off from the Empire entirely, from the British not at all, if I want India to gain and not to grieve. The emperorship must go and I should love to be an equal partner with Britain sharing her joys and sorrows and equal partnership on equal terms." He expected that conscientious people of the world would extend support to strengthen his struggle against the organised violence of the State. Though Gandhi could not ever plan his visit to the United States, the then US President Roosevelt still sent his envoy to meet Gandhi during his fast in Poona and mediate with the government. When the envoy was not allowed to do so, the President expressed his deep concern over the political crisis in India and hoped that some solution might be discovered to prevent worsening of the situation.

The response time of even good managers to react to changes in the environment-political, economic, social and technological – is never the same. It may vary from few days to few years. There is also a class of managers who decides and fixes certain parameters and key indicators – measurable directly or indirectly by quantity, number or

---

11. Op. cit. *Mahatma Gandhi - A Great life in Brief*, p.143

quality – such that the threshold levels of these indicators caution them to prepare for and cope with the changing environment appropriately. Finally, there is another breed of maverick managers who fit in the frame, those who do not wait for things to happen, but rather make things happen. This is the class patterned by an autono-mous-strategic behaviour.

Gandhi possessed a blend of all the above managerial characteristics, but events of his life indicate that he was moving from one stage to another with time, as he gained more and more experience in public life. Finally, he turned out to be an autonomous strategist. An extract[12] from his note substantiates that such paradigm shift did take place in his planning: "Our actions were deliberately intended to bring about this result. The underlying purpose of the struggle is to see that at every step the government places itself in a false position. It is designed to expose its autocratic ways."

Adopting, altering or abandoning a particular course of action depending on available and reliable human and material resources – internal or external – is nothing but a strategy. Always bartering for tangible gains is not wise and insisting on getting immediate results is not foresightedness. He believed that when a conflict is resolved, there should be no rancour left in the relation-ship. Getting an opponent even partially convinced on one's viewpoint is a strategic prelude to victory. A historical meeting of Gandhi with Lord Irwin confirms this. After each round of discussion held, Gandhi consulted his peer group during the break and apprised the

---

12. Op.cit. *Test for Ahmedabad and Surat*

members of the outcome of his sitting each time. The Gandhi-Irwin pact, signed on March 5, 1931, made no stipulation about the future of India, but it restored peace in terms that political prisoners would be released, salt would be freely available along the coast and quid pro-quo civil disobedience would be called off. For the first time, an Indian leader and an English dignitary showed mutual regard as equals and discussed issues and conditions across the board. Another significant outcome of this meeting was that the Indian National Congress could make representation at the Second Round Table Conference which served as an open forum for Gandhi to make it clear to all participants that the Indian Congress wanted complete Independence for India. It was Gandhi's strategic victory, moving one step further towards the goal.

It is true that issues of national and international importance have to be broadly deliberated upon by representatives of different political parties and also vetted on the basis of public opinion. But the process of taking decisions on issues of strategic importance cannot be stalled unduly, and cannot be decided to everyone's satisfaction. Though Gandhi approved of a consultative approach and democratic methods to reach a consensus, he also warned that democracy cannot be run if everyone starts meddling with the final stage of the decision-making process set by the leaders. In this sense, he was neither an autocrat nor a democrat, and liked neither the heat of autocracy nor the lull of democracy.

By adding honesty and transparency to his strategic management and treating his adversary with deference, Gandhi made a confluence of two divergent views, and

thus ushered in a new domain of managerial artifact —
ethical strategy. There should be then no mistake if I view
Gandhi as an ethical strategist.

WELFARE MANAGEMENT: SOME IMPORTANT ASPECTS

9

"Let no one try to justify the glaring differences between the classes and masses, the prince and pauper by saying that former needs more. That will be idle sophistry and travesty of my argument."
—Mahatma Gandhi

*

By conferring the Nobel Prize in Economics for the year 1998 upon Professor Amartya Sen, the Nobel Prize Committee has reiterated that human welfare is an important goal of modern economics. A new stream – welfare economics – has thus emerged and brought to the centre stage of management and social sciences. The subject encompasses a range of issues: illiteracy, poverty, famine, healthcare and quality of life. Conventional economics based on market forces ever pushing for consumerism, materialism and accumulation of wealth, has been failing to provide any pragmatic solution to the multiplying problems of mass-deprivation, increased disparity between classes, economic mess, cost and time overrun in projects, and neglect of the weaker sections.

The first requirement of welfare management is food safety management, primarily the responsibility of a government towards its people. Droughts and floods may cause acute food shortage, but may not be the sole cause of famine. Economic bankruptcy and low purchasing power of money have also triggered famine at many places, even though there was food surplus in neighbouring towns and states. Famines (2000-2001) in the states of Rajasthan, Maharashtra and Madhya Pradesh in India are the cases in hand to corroborate this thesis. The USA also reeled under severe economic crunch during the Great Depression period of 1929-1933 due to unprecedented technological unemployment compounded with stiff competition in farm produce. A large population of workers was laid off country wide, and the real income of those in jobs plummeted to almost 50 per cent. The prices of agricultural goods were perpetually declining and farmers were finding it hard to compete in the open market. When loans and subsidies extended to farmers failed to improve their condition, the government resorted to inflation and contraction of farm production, to maintain parity in prices of agricultural and manufactured goods. But unemployment and inflation together made conditions bad to worse, and struck middle class consumers adversely. This created scarcity of food and bred a spectre of famine, and millions loomed on the verge of starvation. Though agricultural produce was available in surplus, people did not have enough money to buy it. It was the Wagner Act (1935) that gave them some respite and a promise for the future.

In the erstwhile USSR too, economic rundown was prominently visible in the late 1980s. Long queues at ration shops, acute shortage of medicines in hospitals and limited supply chain of distribution were key indicators of deteriorating conditions. Centralised authority, huge expenditure on defense programmes, unorganised enterprises, severe restriction on free trade and commerce and state-controlled information flow, were also factors contributing to the breakdown of management order. This eventually triggered a wave of regimentation and segmentation which gained momentum with Gorbachev's ideology of Perestroika and Glasnost, leading ultimately to the disintegration of the USSR into many separate independent Republics (1991).

The welfare policy of a nation is closely related to its social, economic and political agenda and the readiness of its people to adapt to the changes within and outside the system. Since the process is often governed by the prevailing ethos in society, the concept of welfare management in terms of food safety, healthcare, economic equity, education, and dispensation of justice, receives attention in correspondence with the values that a nation nurtures and upholds. Hence, the selection of proper welfare and social policies and their effective implementation is possible only when a nation learns to practice ethics and develop an ethos for the respect of human values. Oligarchic supremacy and autocratic bureaucracy – often insensitive to people's problems – are unable to provide timely redressal of grievances. Complex rules and regulations, procedural delays, unsavoury intermediaries and huge slack time in plan activities can notoriously kill the purpose of any welfare policy.

Economic reforms have failed to bring about social reforms, but social reforms have produced economic reforms, stresses Prof Amartya Sen. What is therefore needed is to formulate suitable social policies to narrow down social disparity, mitigate gender inequality and empower the less privileged. That the welfare management philosophy of Gandhi intersects largely with the domain of Amartya Sen's welfare economics, is evidenced from a statement of the former Vice President of India, late Hon'ble Krishna Kant, in his address at the special convocation function on January 2, 1999 organised by Jawaharlal Nehru University (JNU), New Delhi, to confer Doctor of Letters (Honoris Causa) upon Prof. Amartya Sen : "No one would have been more pleased by what Professor Sen has to say and comment than Mahatma Gandhi." Gandhi conceptualised 'welfare pluralism' which envisages social and welfare services as the joint responsibility of the State, public and private sectors, and NGOs.

The former Executive Director of UNICEF Jim Grant said[1]: "The day will come when the progress of nations will be judged not by their military or economic strength, not by the splendour of their capital cities and public buildings, but by the well being of their peoples; by their levels of health, nutrition and education; by their opportunities to earn a fair reward for their labours; by their ability to participate in the decisions that affect their lives; by the respect that is shown for their civil and political liberties; by the provision that is made for those who are vulnerable and disadvantaged; and by the protection that is afforded to the growing minds and bodies of their children."

---

1. UN Newsletter Gim Grant, Nov.2000, UN information Centre, New Delhi

THE ROLE OF EDUCATION IN EMPOWERMENT

Education, formal, informal and non-formal, is a driving force in all sided developments – moral, social, economic, intellectual and technological. It is also a force to liberate people from many restrictions associated with inaccessibility to information and inability to communicate, both of which can be effectively taken care of by the ability to at least read and write elementary education. In a report titled Treasure Within and submitted to UNESCO, the International Commission on Education for the 21st Century[2] described four basic purposes of education: learning to know, learning to do, learning to be and learning to live together. While expounding the contents of the report, Dr Karan Singh, former Education Minister of India and the only Asian on the Commission, semantically pointed out in a lecture delivered by him in April 1999 at IGNO University, New Delhi, that the Commission had expressed its views in tune with the Indian philosophy of Gyan Yoga (garner knowledge), Karma Yoga (do thy duties), Atma Yoga (know thyself) and Sarva Vasudhaiva Kutumbkam (all human beings of this planet belong to one family).

This concatenates the purpose of 'being', 'learning' and 'knowing' that Gandhi practiced and pleaded with the student community all through. Though preoccupied with national and international issues, his concern for imparting useful education for the overall development of students never waned. He was opposed to Macaulay's approach in setting up educational institutions just to produce a battery of enslaved clerks-British in thinking

---

2. Delor's Commission Report after the World Conference on Higher Education, 5-9 October, 1998, Paris

and British in loyalty – for routine work at government offices. He always considered education as a tool for shaping both career and conduct, and an instrument for building a moral character, hence a balanced human being with values and ethical entrepreneurialism. He was convinced that education plays a very vital role in the integrated development of mind and body, and hence it is an important constituent of welfare management. Information gleaned by students must be translated into knowledge, and knowledge into wisdom. They must understand the purpose of their learning and develop competence to apply knowledge critically, so as to be able to see and draw up an orderly pattern even in the chaos. Thus education must make people wise, work-oriented, creative, constructive and compassionate. Gandhi once said[3]: "Money given for the purpose of education is no philanthropy; it is the investment of best kind."

Education must also train people to live together in such symbiosis, that each individual participates in the sustainable development of the community and the nation. Sabarmati Ashram in India, Phoenix settlement near Durban, and Tolstory farm outside Johannesburg set up by Gandhi, are exemplars of community centres. There, norms and rules were stringent and their enforcement was strict. People at these centres learnt about dignity of labour, collaborative work, entrepreneurialism and community living based on collective vision and shared responsibilities. The significance of setting up these ashrams and farms for community development was more or less the same as visualised now by the United Nations which

---

defines[4] community development as "the process by which the efforts of people themselves are united with those of government authorities to improve the economic, social and cultural conditions of communities, to integrate these communities into the life of the nation enabling them to contribute fully to national progress". To fulfill social and moral obligations towards the community through education, Gandhi stressed that "our children should not be taught as to despise labour". No work should be considered infra dignitatem; class differentiation made on this basis is not only meaningless but also the root cause of class war.

While teachers and students are main stakeholders in the education sector, they are also the main players in the long term planning of a country. They influence social and economic policies and are themselves influenced by social and economic changes. Consequently, training of teachers and retraining of trainers in accordance with the needs of a society and demands of the domestic and international markets, has to be an ongoing process. Through his addresses in schools, colleges and universities, Gandhi continued his interaction both with students and teachers, highlighting the importance of the public good characteristic of elementary, secondary, vocational and higher education.

At the inauguration of Gujarat Vidyapeeth in 1920, he delivered an inaugural address as its Chancellor. He gave key-note address in 1921 on the foundation day of Kashi Vidyapeeth, and also at the convocation of the Banaras Hindu University in 1942. Gandhi considered education

---

4. CYP Module 9, Commonwealth Secretariat Publication, London, May 1998.

as the prime mover in the process of empowerment, hence brought in focus the educational need of disadvantaged groups. In 1919, he opened for a school for backward class children in Ahmedabad (Gujarat) and in 1921 inaugurated the first national school (Lokmanya Rashtriya Kanya Pathshala) for girls in Bombay. Being deeply concerned with the problems of physically challenged children, he spoke on this issue in 1928 at the school for deaf and dumb in Ahmedabad. At the inauguration of the crafts block at National School, Vile Parle, Bombay, he stressed the need of vocational training and courses. He also interacted with the student community of Eton, Oxford, Nottigham and Cambridge.

The process of social reforms and welfare management is not hurdle-free. There are many bottlenecks and a crucial one amongst them is illiteracy. Again, I find no better exposition on the subject than that given by Prof Sen in his speech upon receiving the Giovanni Agnelli International Prize. He said that illiteracy is not just lack of freedom to read and write, but also the curtailment of many other freedoms that are contingent upon communication that requires at least reading and writing. Damage done to a nation and also to society due to the callous handling of educational programmes and policies is not quickly visible; it is visible only after a few decades when the damage has already cracked the moral and social fabric so deep and wide, that crimes and criminals like volcanic lava start swarming and swallowing the society.

There is no dispute that automation does accelerate the process of industrial growth and development in a country, hence the economic condition of its people. But the scenario of pre-independent India points to the then government's harsh attitude towards the poor and the peasantry, and its programmes to continue uninhibited exploitation of natural resources of the country. Had the policies been conducive and rightly implemented for the welfare of the society – which was then mostly agrarian – Gandhi would have been much less critical of automation and industrialisation. Unfortunately, wherever automation was adopted, and industries were set up, workers were faced with miserable conditions. He, therefore, pleaded that workers be treated as humans and not as machinery spare parts. While addressing the audience at the inaugural session of the International Round Table on Mobilisation, Participation and Development – Old Issues and New Challenges at Jamia Hamdard University, New Delhi, March 13-15, 2000, Justice V.R. Krishna Iyer (Retd. Justice, Supreme Court of India) said: "In the name of globalisation, corporate carnivorism is on the rise; we see assassination of men by men only. It was the great man Gandhi who advocated the economics where man matters."

ECONOMIC EQUITY STABILISER – TRUST AND TRUSTEESHIP

Economic equality of all is practically impossible to achieve. But economic equity should not be out of reach. Which means that there is a fair and impartial distribution of wealth so that every one has enough to meet one's basic needs and is able to lead life with dignity. These needs include proper food, shelter, education and primary healthcare for all. Being strongly opposed to extravagance and supercilious display of wealth, Gandhi cautioned[5]:

---

5. *Harijan*, June 3, 1939.

"Let no one try to justify the glaring differences between the classes and masses, the prince and pauper, by saying that the former needs more. That will be idle sophistry and travesty of my argument." Perhaps, his apprehension that he might still be misinterpreted led him to define economic equity (not economic equality I believe) further in the rigid frame of morality[6]: "If a single man demanded as much as a man with wife and children, that would be violation of economic equality." However, the requirements of a person or a group may sometimes be realistic, hence should not always be attributed to greed and passion. But if these requirements are shown as a non-detachable tag of status – social, economic or political – they are subjective and superficial and the root cause of class war. Again, the requirements of some individuals or groups may be circumstantial or situational, and the demand for appropriately more could be justifiable on the ground of genuine reasons, but such cases have to be treated on the basis of merit alone and should be carefully prioritised against the needs of the common man. On seeing the colossal expenditure lavished upon so called VIPs and VVIPs for their travel, fun and food, Gandhi must have been saddened, and must have perceived it to happen again; hence he took an ideal view of economic equity and conceived a plan for its implementation by creating the concept of Trust and Trusteeship. He elaborated on this point[7]: "Supposing I have come to acquire fair amount of wealth either by way of legacy, or by means of trade and industry. I must know that all that wealth does not belong to me. What belongs to me is the right to an honourable

---

6. Ibid.

7. Ibid.

livelihood, no better than that enjoyed by millions of others. The rest of my wealth belongs to the community and must be used for the welfare of the community."

It would be, however, very difficult for a capitalist or an industrialist to instantly relish Gandhi's theory of Trusteeship which seeks a paradigm shift in the philosophy of life. It needs strong will and great moral courage to renounce one's legal title of ownership on wealth, earned by the self or inherited by legacy, and then to accept mere custodianship of the same. But the concept of Trusteeship, no doubt, offers a dependable means for promoting economic equity in a society.

Nowadays, a counterpart of capitalists in the guise of people's representatives has come to barge into the democratic institutions like Assembly and Parliament. One can also watch live on TV their playful presence in parliamentary sessions and meetings of statutory bodies. And soon you notice that there are many jokers, shrieking and sneaking, squabbling and squirming, creating a pandemonium. A common man whose basic needs have not been fulfilled for years, would, on viewing this, be reacting with hatred and hopelessness. One would also naturally develop ill will against those white-clad fatties and gold-goggled snobs stepping out of meeting without transacting any business of public interest.

Alfred Ford, a philanthropist and great grandson of Henry Ford of Ford Motors, is reported to have expressed[8], while discussing social and spiritual projects in Kolkata: "Wealth is a gift from God. It's best if it is used to help others and

---

8. *The Times of India*, December 8, 2003.

serve HIM ultimately.

No industry operates in vacuum; it draws resources from society. Hence, it must fulfill its social and societal obligations. Industrialists and business magnates must help workers and labourers improve their economic conditions and quality of life. Against this backdrop, Gandhi worked on the idea of Trust and Trusteeship. He was against capitalism that philosophises unrestrained amassing of wealth at the expense of abject poverty of others. But he was not against capitalists as he wrote[9] in *Young India*: "By the non-violent methods, we seek not to destroy the capitalist; we seek to destroy capitalism [...] And if I would recognise the fundamental equality, as I must, of the capitalist and the labour, I must not aim at his destruction." If 'capital' is to be considered as an engine to start an industrial activity, 'worker' is to be regarded as a force to carry it out. Capital and labour are complementary as well as supplementary to each other. One cannot fully replace the other. Gandhi tries to explain the same in a people-friendly language[10]: "If he [the worker] aims at becoming the sole owner, he will most likely be killing the goose that lays the golden eggs. Inequalities in intelligence and even opportunities will last till the end of time." He further elaborates: "What I expect of you therefore is that you should hold all your riches as a Trust to be used solely in the interest of those who sweat for you, and to whose industry and labour you owe all your position and prosperity. I want to make your labourers co-partners of your wealth," Here, Gandhi does not aim at depriving capitalists of their wealth; he pleads

9. *Young India*, March 26, 1931.

10. Ibid.

for co-partnership of labourers in the industry's wealth. Implicit in this is the concept of shared profit and shared risk as once pronounced by Akio Morita, co-founder of Sony. If a company is sick or its business is in recession, the workers will have to reconcile with the appropriately minimum payment for sustenance and the capitalists shall have to provide relief to the workers till assets last. In all fairness, Gandhi pleaded for workers' right to access information about the functioning of the company or mill, as made clear in the following[11]: "It is vital to the well-being of industry that the workmen should be regarded as equals with the shareholders and that they have, therefore, every right to possess an accurate knowledge of the transactions of the mills." However, one also cannot deny the fact that the investor's capital used in setting up an industry, and management's expertise in business operations are crucially important in stabilising a profitable business. Therefore, they too deserve a share of proportionate reward and a vote of authority commensurate to their capability and responsibility – a legitimate claim that should not be ignored. Further, it is not wholly correct to say that corporate groups are averse to human considerations and opposed to employees' rights while State-controlled enterprises and organisations are people-oriented soft peddlers. The fact is that State ownership is not always a ready solution to eradicating the ills of private ownership. Gandhi analyses the two critically in the following[11]: "State ownership is better than private ownership. But that too is objectionable on the ground of violence. The State represents violence in a concentrated and organised form. And the fear is always there that the

---

11. *Young India*, December 5, 1929.

State may use too much violence against those who differ from it."

For the good health of an organisation, capitalists, bureaucrats and workers have to work in harmony and feel concerned for each other. Malicious enjoyment in the crisis of others and mischievous maneuvering for exploitation would be atrocious, provocative and mutually ruinous. It is, therefore, essential to create an environment of mutual trust, respect and harmony.

OBJECT ORIENTED MANAGEMENT THROUGH APPROPRIATE METHODS, MEANS AND PRACTICES (OOMTAMP)

10

"The method alone interests me, and by method
I mean the agency through which the wishes of
the people are reached. There are only two methods:
one is that of fraud and force, and the
other is that of non-violence and truth.
—Mahatma Gandhi

*

Profit margin – huge or small – is the keystone of any business, trade, commerce or industry. Any debate on morality cannot ignore this ground reality. In fair trade, developing countries often take stance on moral issues and ethical practices which are conveniently overlooked and overridden by developed countries. When George Bush Jr. stressed, soon after taking over as US President, that "free trade is a moral imperative", it created a stir amongst corporate groups to search for a new order in business and trade. Whether the elements of morality or ethicality are required to be observed, partly or wholly, in fair trade or free trade, or in both, is a subject that needs consideration on a wide range of issues and calls for a global perspective. The former Prime Minister of India, A.B. Vajpayee, discussed with the then Singaporean President the prospects of entering into a free trade agreement[1]. Since new market and new business will always raise the question of fair trade' and free trade, and since votaries of either have already recognised morality as a necessary obligation in trade and business, it ought to be given its due place. Therefore, the first thing to practice both in fair and free trade is truthfulness, so that the interest of all nations and societies is reasonably well served. This could be possible only when one does not infringe on the rights of others and is conscious of one's responsibilities and obligations – a basic principle treasured in the lessons of morality and ethicality. It may surprise and intrigue many – in business and politics to know that Gandhi, during his stay in Pretoria, made his first public speech[2] in 1893-94 on "truthfulness in business".

Even though there is only a diffused boundary line between morality and ethicality, some distinction can still be made: morals are often appended with austerity and sanctity, which may have different meanings in different religions and customs, whereas ethics is taken to mean a framework of logically sound and just principles of humanity and human values defining a code of non-intrusive and non-exploitive conduct. Ethical standards may also sometimes differ and be relative. Still, a crude form of it taken even from the primitive era, would speak

---

1. *The Times of India*, January 5, 2003.

2. *'Mahatma Gandhi - A Chronology'* compiled by K.P. Goswami. Publication Division Ministry of Information & Broadcasting, GOI, 1971:

something good and humane. Above all, ethical standards
must pass a "test of reasonableness" and equity. Hence,
distribution of benefits to all direct or indirect stakeholders in any plan, programme, business, trade or
agreement has to be assessed ethically and justly. Given
this dimension of ethicality, issues related to the propriety
of resources and means (man, money, methods, material,
markets etc) are absolutely important. They need to be
thrashed out and addressed simultaneously under the
generic term 'proper means' and 'practices'.

If the world recognises sustainable development as the
necessity of today and responsibility towards posterity,
management by objectives (MBO) and result-oriented
performance appraisal (ROPA), are not enough to regulate
ethics in business, because they do not reflect any aspect
of the propriety of means. Almost all schools of
management thought and their proponents have been
cleverly evading this issue of propriety and ethicality of
means and methods in achieving the goals. In all
management approaches so far known, it is the end success
in terms of profit and position occupy centre stage.

Peter F. Drucker, celebrity in the field, describes management as a multipurpose organ that manages a business,
manages managers and manages workers and work. He
maintains a conspicuous silence on the subject of morality
and ethicality in business and remains non-committal to
its attributes. He appears to have granted his managers
unlimited freedom to apply any method and use any
means to deliver the end result – profit; then find any
justification aposteriori. The definition of 'management'
that rhetorically uses 'manager', 'manage' and 'manage',

keeps ethics dangling and provides unbounded and unguarded scope for the interpretation of ethics in management.

L.A. Appley focuses on the efforts of other people in attaining goals when he argues "management is the accomplishment of results through the efforts of other people." By 'other people', he obviously means workers, first line supervisors, junior and middle-level managers directly responsible for the execution of work, operation of machines and distribution of goods and services. In such organisations, the laurels of success are shared by the top management, and failures are dumped on the workers, supervisors, junior and middle management cadres.

Stanley Vance's perception is that "management is simply the process of decision making and control over the action of other human beings for the express purpose of attaining predetermined goals is a logical fallacy, as it creates a rift between the top management and other staff in the organisation. To have authority to make decisions without sharing responsibilities violates one-to-one correspondence between authority and responsibility which is necessary for good governance, since someone controlling the actions of others without oneself being accountable is more like a thief policing other thieves."

Curiously so, Koontz and O'Donnell build a management-wizard crafty enough to "get things done through people and also the informally organised groups." Unless a manager presents himself/herself as a role model, getting things properly done by others is neither easy nor workable in the long run. Furthermore, informally organised groups who would work for the top management are most likely to seek gratification in one way or the other. And if the management entertains their interference in the system and obliges them, they are sure to turn into brokers or into a caucus, keeping management insular towards staff and surroundings, held up for unpleasant ransom.

John F. Mee presents another definition of management which makes tall claims for extraordinary results, perhaps too incongruous: "Management may be defined as the art of securing maximum results with minimum efforts so as to secure maximum prosperity and happiness for both employer and employees and give the public best possible services." How can these two mutually opposite objectives be met? In a competitive business world, only minimum efforts by management cannot maximise the desired results. And, if minimum efforts can maximise gains, clients, customers and public in general cannot be given the best product or the best service. Yes, they can be surely duped. Unless accredited and standardised, the phrase 'best possible' so artfully used may prove to be the 'worst possible' for others, as many nasties and crooked in this world make their heaven on the hell of millions of the poor.

Thus the credos of most corporates revolve around 'getting work done by others', 'getting maximum results by putting in minimum efforts', 'managing man and machine', etc. There could be no worse abuse of the meaning of management than that contained in these definitions percolating down from time to time in books written for management graduates. If this is what our future managers have to learn from their many years of studies and training, there is no reason as to why they should not abet their corporate employers in amassing wealth by any means, and why they should not evade norms, rules and regulations meant for the enforcement and promotion of fair deal, equity and equitability in society? To understand management by repeatedly going through such crass phrases as these, which utterly disregard the importance of 'means', is detrimental to any system and society. It would also set a sharkonian trend in business where big magnates will swallow the small ethical entrepreneurs.

Though Japanese management philosophy does take care of employees' welfare, there are still no clear-cut views on the propriety of means and methods in business. But there are obvious cases of some world class corporates which do generate huge revenue, yet their shareholders, clients and vendors hold them in high esteem because a desirable degree of ethicality is maintained in their business operations. IBM, Sony, Intel, Texas Instruments, Infosys and Tata, are a few well known cases quoted by many market research journals. They stay atop not just by playing ducks and drakes with their clients and customers, but by assuring them of the quality of their products and services, and by continually searching for some novel methods of value addition. As far as the question of 'skimming' the price at certain point of time is concerned, everyone has the right to sell one's patent, product or services at high price, if there are takers in the fair market.

Although acquisition, merger, joint-venture, division and partnership have become a common deal in today's corporate world, ethical practices can still be continued in all ventures and alliances. While competitors under threat may allege others of oligopolistic nexus and charge each other with monopolistic and restrictive trade practices, they must ensure that in their own business, ethicality does not become a casualty. The majority of corporates and top managers consider ethicality in industry, trade, or business as an antithesis to profit making. And it has been their conscious effort to instill the philosophy of 'end justifies the means' in the minds of young managers even if it means a Faustian deal, economic ravage and social cleavage of the very system in which they are operating and drawing resources from. Many believe that as long as fraudulent methods and unfair means do not pose threat to the organisation, one may have them continued. Perhaps, for attaining the goal in the shortest possible time, conscience is overpowered by temptation for success and righteousness of the means takes very often the backseat. If Machiavellian epithet – end justifies the means – goes so deep in the psyche of managers in all cadres that no means, if it can be just a pointer to success, shall be considered as corrupt, then the social system is surely heading to a catastrophe which will take its toll on human and social values and also the country's economy. The erstwhile conditions in Iraq, Iran and Afghanistan are glaring examples that value erosion and social anarchy spiral down growth and development, and lead to economic crisis.

Smithsonian approach in business may work in accelerating economic development in some exclusive situations only when each individual, business group and organisation is conscious of one's obligations towards other competitors and the society as well. But where each and every one is running amuck to reach the top and amass wealth by hook or by crook, Smithsonian approach would utterly fail and do more harm than good. Even in large democracies, where individual entrepreneurs, companies and firms are considerably free to carry out their business operations, results are not fail-proof. Although by using various legal instruments, a State government or Central government can make intervention and regulate business, trades and industries, perfidious MNCs and perjurious business groups may still remain unflinching and unaffected. The agents of their management tunnel through the power corridors of government departments and make access, through information brokers, to crucial and classified policy documents.

Consequently, they get a big lead time to activate their new strategies and frame policies to counter the government's intervention and turn it to their benefit, while others keep waiting for official announcements and communications. The vicious cycle repeats itself. The rich one, flouting norms and procedures, is finally a winner, while law-abiding entrepreneur or struggler is ultimately a loser. This eventually slows down multi-level and multi-dimensional social development, and hampers the overall economic growth of a country.

No industry or business works in vacuum. It has to draw its major resources from society and the country in which it operates. And if business objectives have intrinsic merits and management does not ignore its societal responsibilities, management has to draw conscientiously a line between ethicality and unethicality. Corporates and MNCs which are outsourcing their work to other countries, may still fail to take it seriously. For long lasting overall development, a government has to frame such policies in respect of industries, trade and commerce, that the welfare of the State and its people is not bruised, and the importance of means and methods is not belittled. Any policy – social or economic – needs to be amended and reviewed if it deviates from its objectives and purpose, or appears to be straying from the use of right means. Welfare of the State was no doubt supreme in the mind of Gandhi, but he did not separate it from the welfare of people. This is fairly well reflected in his socio-economic policies.

A problem with the majority of managers is that they find it too difficult to configure a profitable plan for their business, trade or industry with ethical means and methods. It should be remembered here that there are standard meanings of the word 'ethicality' and 'propriety of means' which are the same in all religions, cultures, customs and civil codes, hence one need not stretch them too far or pull them too low to support one's misconceived or misguided interpretation.

Setting high goals, wanting success and having ambition to excel per se are not evils. Competition and struggle are not bad but rather a necessity, because they make life creative, innovative, enduring and enterprising. But if, in competing against each other, one loses sight of ethicality and sanctity of means and methods, one may turn devilish with obsession of achieving success and fulfilling one's ambitions.

A survey report[3] prepared jointly by Montgomery and

---

3. 'Corporate Social Responsibility - Reputation Effects on MBAs Job Choices', Montgomery, David and Catherine, Ramus, Stanford Graduate School of Business (GSB) Research Paper #1805, May 2003, Available on gsbinfo@gsb.stanford.edu April 2, 2004.

Catherine on the job selection attributes that influence job choices of MBAs, shows a new and emerging trend. The report covered interviews of about 800 MBAs of leading North American universities, and was concluded in 2003. It is stated therein that the major incentive conventionally for an MBA to join a company has been financial and only financial. So by giving more pay and perquisites to these MBAs, any company could easily hire them, CEOs believed. The report however, further reveals that now a new generation of MBAs even from top institutions are willing to forgo on an average 12 to 20 per cent of their income in order to work for companies that have a reputation for high ethical standards and caring for employees and community. Eventually, corporate governance has to seriously ponder over and redefine corporate ethics.

It is true that the degree of success in reaching goals is an important determinant of the efficiency of management. But if the means used in the process are against the canons of humanity and disastrous to humankind, success in all its forms is condemnable and contemptible. The world has not forgotten that a master plan of few disguised terrorists to engineer Kamikaze blast of two civilian aircrafts, on September 11, 2001, by deflecting them to ram into the World Trade Centre (WTC) in New York, USA, a country with highest defense surveillance. This resulted in thousand of deaths and in thousands being maimed. In July 2005, London was also rocked by a series of blasts. One can certainly say that these are the cases of highly efficient and effective management. But, is that really quotable? Whether world class managers would also agree to act secretively or lend their support overtly or covertly in the elimination or suppression of theirs or other's competitors by using equally contemptible methods and means? Should the manager class be so pliable as to execute any order of their boss, in utter disregard to ethical and human values?

For Gandhi, the sanctity and propriety of methods and means was no less important than the justness of cause. Since all operations and methods use means (which could be a thing or an activity), the rightness of means and methods is an inter-related concept. When asked about his views on the form of democracy he perceived, Gandhi's sagacious reply[4] was: "I do not know; the method alone interests me, and by method I mean the agency through which the wishes of the people are reached. There are only two methods; one is that of fraud and force, and the other is that of non-violence and truth." He further elucidates that exteriorly means may not appear corrupt, but intrinsically, they may be ruinous to society at large. His emphasis on the purity of means, methods and goals has one or the same propose[5]: "There is just the same inviolable connection between the means and the end as there is between the seed and the tree."

This is what I call object-oriented management through appropriate methods, means and practices (OOM TAMP), and this is what would lead to the omega (w) state – the highest point in the orderly functioning of management. This is to be adopted voluntarily in our practices, since it cannot be enforced by any legislation. A conscious decision has to be taken by corporate groups that methods and means used by them to earn profit and promote business

---

4. *Young India*, April 24, 1930

5. 'Hindi Swaraj or Indian Home Rule', p.71 (*Navjivan* 1958 Ahmedabad)

conform to ethical norms and standards which are globally shared and valued. This has to go into the psyche of managers, has to be rooted primarily in the conscience and has to be reflected in their actions. Only then business and trade can be made free from fraud, force, falsity and deception.

"The greatest omission in our 106 year history is undoubtedly that Mahatma Gandhi never received the Nobel Peace prize. Gandhi could do without the Nobel Peace Prize. Whether Nobel committee can do without Gandhi is the question."

—Geir Lundestad
Secretary, Norwegian Nobel Committee
(The Times Of India, October 17, 2006)

ABOUT THE AUTHOR

Dr. RAM PRATAP,
Ph. D. (Mgmt); Ph.D. (Phys)

Having obtained his M.Sc. (Physics) from the University of Allahabad and Ph.D. (Physics) from the Banaras Hindu University, in 1974, Dr Ram Pratap joined as faculty member of the PG department of physics, University of Bombay, where he became Professor in 1985 and Chairman, Department of Physics, in 1993. During this period, he guided many research scholars for their doctoral degree in physics and applied science, and published about 30 papers in national and international journals. Many appeared in journals published from the UK and Germany, and a few others were presented during international conferences at the University of California Berkeley.

During his tenure at the University of Bombay, Dr Pratap earned his second doctorate degree in management. In this field, he has to his credit about 20 papers, lectures and presentations at seminars and symposia. The first comprehensive paper on performance appraisal of academics was authored by him and it was published in the UGC Journal of Higher Education in 1985. He has also been a visiting faculty of management for several years.

In 1994, Dr Pratap was Director of the G. Institute of Career Education and Development (vocational/professional studies) under the governance of Bombay University. The institute offers inter-alia diploma programs in computer software, environment pollution control, journalism (English, Hindi and Marathi), travel and tourism etc.

In 1998, Dr Pratap moved to open and distance education and joined the Indira Gandhi National Open University in New Delhi as Director for planning and development. He was responsible for the preparation of annual and five year plans (9th and 10th), budgeting, securing funds from GOI, launching of new programmes, academic audits, best practices, MIS, database and manpower requirement forecasting and planning. The HRD Ministry, GOI, entrusted him with the very prestigious project 'Educational Development of the Northeastern Region' with a grant of Rs 15 cr. The project included setting up of an IT network in all Northeastern states and the utilisation of indigenous resources for the promotion of small scale industries.

In 2003-2004, Dr Pratap took over as Special Officer (State Universities), Governor's Secretariat, Patna (Bihar). The responsibilities included constant interaction with functionaries in higher education, participation in policy making and planning, implementation of State university Acts and Statutes, TQM in education and effective use of emerging technologies.

Gandhian Management
The Paragon of Higher Order Management
Dr Ram Pratap